DRUGS, LAW AND THE STATE

DRUGS, LAW AND THE STATE

Edited by

Harold H. Traver
Mark S.Gaylord

Transaction Publishers
New Brunswick (U.S.A.) and London (U.K.)

This hardback edition first published in the United States in 1992
by Transaction Publishers, New Brunswick, New Jersey 08903
in collaboration with Hong Kong University Press
is distributed only in North America and South America.

Library of Congress Cataloging-in-Publication Data

Drugs, law, and the state/edited by Harold H. Traver, Mark S. Gaylord.
p. cm.
Includes bibliographical references and index.
ISBN 1-56000-082-1 (cloth): $32.95
1. Narcotics, Control of —cross-cultural studies.   2. Drug traffic—Cross-
cultural studies.   3. Drug abuse—Cross-cultural studies.
I. Traver, Harold.   II. Gaylord, Mark S.
HV5801.D773   1992
363.4'5—dc20
92-23926
CIP

Printed in Hong Kong

Contents

Contributors

Harold H. Traver is a Lecturer in Sociology at The University of Hong Kong. He founded, in 1986, The University of Hong Kong's postgraduate program in criminology. He received a Ph.D. from the University of California-Santa Barbara in 1973. His research interests include policing, organized crime, and drug policy. He is co-editor (with Jon Vagg) of *Crime and Justice in Hong Kong*, and author of journal articles on crime and economic development.

Mark S. Gaylord is a Senior Lecturer in Sociology at the City Polytechnic of Hong Kong, where he has been a member of staff since 1987. He received a Ph.D. in sociology from the University of Missouri-Columbia in 1984. His interests include criminology and the sociology of law. He is co-author (with John F. Galliher) of *The Criminology of Edwin Sutherland*. He is currently editing a book on Hong Kong's criminal justice system.

William J. Chambliss is a Professor of Sociology at George Washington University. He received a Ph.D. from Indiana University in 1962, and has taught at the University of Washington, the University of California-Santa Barbara, and the University of Delaware. He has held visiting professorships at the University of Ibadan, Nigeria; the University of Uppsala; the London School of Economics; and the University of Wisconsin. In 1968-69 he was Staff Sociologist, Task Force on Law and Law Enforcement, President's Commission of Violence. Dr. Chambliss was elected President of the American Society of Criminology in 1988. He is author or co-author of several books, including: *Crime and Legal Process; Law, Order and Power; On the Take: From Petty Crooks to Presidents; Exploring*

Criminology; and numerous journal articles on law, deviance and crime.

John F. Galliher is a Professor of Sociology at the University of Missouri-Columbia. He received a Ph.D. from Indiana University in 1967. His interests include criminology and the sociology of law. He is the author or co-author of several books, including: *Violence in Northern Ireland: Understanding Protestant Perspectives; Morals Legislation Without Morality; Criminology: Human Rights, Criminal Law and Crime; The Criminology of Edwin Sutherland;* and numerous journal articles.

Jørgen Jepsen is an Associate Professor of Criminology at the University of Arrhus, Denmark. He is Past Secretary General of the Scandinavian Research Council for Criminology. He is currently Chairman of the Danish Alcohol and Drugs Research Initiative, and Board Member of the Center for Alcohol and Drugs Research, University of Arrhus. He has written widely on crime forecasting, corporate crime, and drugs and crime.

Ahti Laitinen is an Associate Professor of Sociology of Law at University of Turku, Finland, and Docent of the Sociology of Law, University of Helsinki. He received the degree of Doctor of Political Science from the University of Turku in 1977. His books include *The Crimes of Power, Social Power and Corruption, Biologism in the Social Sciences,* and *Consumer Protection and Legislation.*

Axel R. Reeg studied law at the University of Munich, the National University of Singapore, and the University of Freiburg, where he received a Ph.D. in 1990. Dr. Reeg was Research Fellow in the Max Planck Institute for International and Foreign Law (1988-1990), served in the Ministry of Justice of the Federal State of Baden-Wurttenberg (1985-1987), and lectured in the Faculty of Law at the University of Freiburg (1988-1990). He is now in private practice in Mannheim, Germany.

Ernesto U. Savona is a Professor of Criminology at the University of Trento, Italy, and served as a Visiting Fellow at the National Institute of Justice, Washington, D.C. He is Senior Scientific Consultant at UNICRI (United Nations Interregional Crime and

Justice Research Institute), in Rome; and is a consultant to the Secretary General of the United Nations on enhancement of the UN's structure for drug abuse control. Prof. Savona has been a visiting scholar at the University of California, Berkeley (1981), Oxford University (1982), the University of Montreal (1984), Yale University (1988), and Cambridge University (1988). His interests are organized crime and the relationship between drugs and crime.

Masayuki Tamura is a psychologist and senior researcher in the Socio-environment Section, Prevention of Crime and Delinquency Division, National Research Institute of Police Science, Tokyo. He received a B.A. and M.A. from the Tokyo Metropolitan University. He is author of many journal articles on drugs, youth gangs, and violence.

Acknowledgments ━━━━━━━━━

This book owes much to the generous assistance of colleagues and friends. Manfred Brusten, Robert G. Andry, Merly Komala and Wong Siu Lun deserve special thanks for their assistance in organizing the conference at which these essays were presented. We owe a great debt also to Karl Schuessler for contributing the Dedication, and to Alan Block for writing the Foreword. Finally, we gratefully acknowledge Samuel R. Gaylord for his seasoned editing skills.

Dedication ━━━━━━━━━━━━━━━━━━━━━━

To Alfred R. Lindesmith, 1905-1991

Alfred R. Lindesmith was born in 1905 on a farm near Owatonna, Minnesota, where he attended public school. At home and at church he acquired a facility in German, including German poetry, which he would recite with little encouragement. In recent times, on leaving him at the convalescent center in Bloomington, Indiana, my "Auf Widersehen" usually brought a smile to his face.

In high school Lindy was an outstanding athlete and his record time in the high hurdles was never broken. He would tell you this and immediately add that the school went out of existence, at least in name, a little while later. He always made sure that no one exaggerated the importance of his accomplishments.

At Carleton College, in Northfield, Minnesota, Lindy was an outstanding student and athlete. He was elected to Phi Beta Kappa and lettered in football. He liked to tell a story about his high mark in geometry. It seems that his professor would prove a Euclidean theorem by having recourse to the term "obvious." For example, "any two sides of a triangle are together greater than the third side. Obvious." Lindesmith used the same expression on the final examination and got an "A" in the course. For him it was a principle that students had a right to play tricks on teachers who in turn played tricks on them.

Before starting his graduate studies in sociology at the University of Chicago in the early 1930s, Lindy took an M.A. in education at Columbia University and taught school one year each in Sleepy Eye, Minnesota, Council Bluffs, Iowa, and at the Stevens Point Teachers' College in Wisconsin. His Ph.D. (1938) came a year later than planned. Lindy was advised by the chair that he would have to take his course in social psychology before he could take preliminary examinations. And so he had to wait for a whole year before being admitted to candidacy. The latitude Lindy so readily accorded students in setting their own paces may have had its origin in his own frustration as a graduate student at Chicago.

Lindesmith joined the department of sociology at Indiana University in 1936, retiring forty years later in 1976. He insisted that no testimonial dinner be held in his honor, but did consent to a departmental cocktail party. In the 1950s and 1960s he was on leave from time to time to accept visiting professorships here and there. In 1965 he was awarded the title of University Professor by Indiana University in recognition of the distinction he had brought to the university. For a while after retirement he drove a Red Cross van, transporting needy people to hospitals and clinics in central Indiana.

Of sociological colleagues I have known through the years, Alfred Lindesmith stands out as one loved by all. What were the traits that so endeared him to others? He was kind and gentle, rather than cold and brusque. He did not look down on people and keep them at bay; he erected no barriers between himself and others. He treated students as equals and was not condescending to them in manner.

Lindy always took people at their word. His premise was that people meant what they said and he always tried to grasp the meaning of their words. He was never insincere and fully expected sincerity in others. Right after World War II, I mentioned that I had no need for a barometer on board ship because I could gauge atmospheric pressure by the pressure on my head. After a while he said that he guessed I was joking, but at first he took me at my word.

Lindy's speech was plain and simple, rather than fancy and complicated. To the degree possible he avoided the jargon of academe, striving always to put his thoughts in plain English. In line with this habit he was never taken in by bombastic writing.

He was no operator. He did not climb the academic ladder by catering to people of power, telling them what they wanted to hear. In the late 1940s he was urged by the younger faculty to stand for the chair after it became vacated by Professor Edwin H. Sutherland. He declined, saying that administrative work was unattractive to him and, besides, he would be an awful administrator. But his name kept coming up whenever the chair became vacant.

Lindy was neat and tidy in personal appearance, but not in the least bit vain. He was self-contained in the sense that he paid no heed to the conventions of fashion. My remembrance is that he had a single blue suit that he wore to funerals; otherwise he dressed in jeans, sweater, and, of course, caps and old shoes.

He was most unpretentious — never pretending to be what he was not. Though he understood that life for many is a masquerade, he wanted no part of that make-believe world. In this regard, he reminded me of Tolstoy's portrayal of the country aristocrats in Russia who shunned the false society of Moscow.

Lindesmith's reputation rests mainly on his studies of drug addiction and his views on how to solve the drug problem. For his views, and to his credit, he was persecuted by the Federal Bureau of Narcotics, the head of which made a trip to Bloomington to investigate Lindy's possible links to the criminal underworld. His writings were instrumental in persuading the American Medical Association to regard drug addiction as disease rather then crime. Until the day he died, he received letters from scientists all over the world acknowledging the influence of his work on their own thinking. In Europe, I was told more than once that Alfred R. Lindesmith was the founder of the sociological approach to drug addiction. Few sociologists have had such an impact on their specialty.

To thousands of university students, Lindesmith is known for his textbook on social psychology (with Anselm Strauss) now in its seventh edition and translated into several languages. It is a safe bet than Lindy's style — informal, casual, free, and easy — has had much to do with the popularity of this book.

On a personal note, he and I tangled now and then about a proper methodology in sociology but we agreed that there was room for differences of opinion and that no one has all the answers. We also agreed that eclecticism would get us nowhere and that it is far better to follow a line to the end rather than skip lightly over many.

Lindy was not himself during the last few years and toward the end there was little that one could do to make him laugh. Among his friends it was thought that he never came back, at least emotionally, after his wife's death in 1985. In the last year or so before his death, he would grin only if I said "let's Indian wrestle" or "flex your biceps, Lindy." But he wanted no sentimental pity. He was blessed with that pride and courage that enables one to bear hardship with grace and dignity. It is sometimes said that when a friend dies, we die a little too. I prefer to think that when our friends die, they go living within us. And so I believe that at least some of Alfred Lindesmith goes on living in all of us.

Karl Schuessler
Bloomington, Indiana
February 17, 1991

Foreword

Alan A. Block

There are few events in recent history that appear so insensible as the covert arming of Iran and the resulting diversion of profits through Swiss, Panamanian, and Cayman Islands banks purportedly to support the Contras in Nicaragua. As the well-known story goes, the Iran action generated enough money to allow U.S. national security agents, particularly Lt. Colonel Oliver North, to fulfill the dream of maintaining the Contras in the field despite what was termed congressional footdragging and the misguided policies of liberals. By privatizing secret activities in both instances, the planners believed they had found a means of circumventing congressional objections, most notably the Boland Amendment.

Much about the Iran/Contra scandal has been discovered and cogently documented by able writers including, most recently, Theodore Draper (1991). But, in fact, the actual shape and full scope of this action are still concealed for obvious reasons. Multi-faceted secret assignments were carried out by key operatives. Official corruption included foreign and domestic profiteering by the so-called North network abetted by U.S. politicians of the highest order. Illicit cocaine earnings intertwined with staggering munitions deals with the Contras and Iran, and also with regular and paramilitary forces throughout South and Central America, the Middle East, South Africa, and the Golden Crescent. There was a sea-change in the relationships among the Executive Office, the Central Intelligence Agency (CIA), and U.S. military intelligence, and a severing of their past more-or-less constitutional connection to the American public.

How this appalling and extraordinarily dangerous situation came about cannot be perceived clearly without the most scrupulous investigation. But one of the natural results of a successful *coup d'etat* is to render the instruments that normally carry out such investigation impotent. Cover-ups and damage control are the order of the day. The goal of congressional careerists is to stay in office and continue their "con." And the Department of Justice, particularly at the highest levels, is now almost completely politicized. How else to explain secret meetings held by bewildered Department of Justice managers lamenting the end of criminal justice as they work under constant, unseemly, illegal political pressure?

But the U.S. is not Romania as it existed under the Ceaceauscu regime, and the government has neither the ability nor perhaps the ambition to manage secret affairs in the old-fashioned way. Unspeakable change is played out under the guise of law. Exceptional actions are "sold" to citizens who are then instructed how to judge them. In this, the quietest of *coups*, common citizens continue to believe they retain the basic elements of control. The great mass of "chumps," as the Washington insiders characterize the American public, are prodded into opinions without the slightest knowledge of hidden intentions and consequences. One of the ways this occurs is through the creation of overarching demonologies: enemies so vast, so capable, and so fundamentally un-American that the public is overawed. With their judgment clouded and passions aroused, nearly anything goes.

In the late twentieth century, the "war on drugs" assumes the role played formerly by the Cold War. The potent stigmatization of drug users understandably overwhelms, given that tens of millions seem to believe that most are black and something less than fully human. American domestic drug policy is clearly double-edged, designed to frighten middle-class white users away from drugs through draconian laws and the creation of an ever larger private interest in surveillance and drug testing. On the other hand, there is a clear mandate to lock up as many black users and dealers as possible, to warehouse them for as long as it takes. There is an interesting series of assumptions built into this policy: those with something to lose can be frightened out of drug use; those with nothing to lose cannot be and therefore must be locked up.

It does not require great intelligence to understand that prisons primarily serve the black population and that prisons are one of America's rural growth industries. Rural counties that once prospered with small farms, mining ventures, and specialized industrial manufacturing now face bleak futures with hope coming in the form of two kinds of waste heaps: prisons and landfills. With relief, county commissioners and others politically responsible for the business of rural America help the political state by welcoming prisons while at the same time rolling out the carpet for some of the nation's sleaziest crooks eager to secure permission for garbage disposal and hazardous waste landfills. Imagine the real prospects for rural high school graduates who want to remain close to their homes, with luck they may become managers of urban human and industrial waste.

It is commonly accepted that narcotics cause some of the nation's worst ills. Anyone can name them: crack babies; the proliferation of AIDS; violent crime; wasted lives. But are these not hopelessly intertwined on a cause-and-effect ladder? Picture productive life without drugs in New York, a state that has lost over 500 000 jobs in the past three years. In the *New York Times,* Sarah Bartlett (1992) reported that this decline was the worst "since records began being kept in 1939." Writing in the *New York Review of Books,* Jason Epstein (1992) catalogued New York City's economic decline and thus its social disintegration. The city once had a "booming industrial economy, based almost entirely on small manufacturing plants exporting a bewildering variety of goods to all corners of the world, [it] had provided opportunity for generations of immigrants." The industrial base is now dead and gone, replaced by a "concentrated service economy, dominated by a few thousand highly paid mandarins." New York's immigrants, however, have not left. Over the last decade while more than 500 000 white citizens departed the city, "520 000 blacks and Hispanics along with 250 000 Asians" moved in.

For those inclined to use the term, consider New York City's "opportunity-structure" and then ponder whether the selling and indeed taking of drugs makes sense. New York, city and state, may of course be substituted with scores of other cities and states and much the same conditions would appear. Washington, D.C., the political and murder capital of the U.S., is another grim example. A recent study by Jerome Miller, the head of the National Center on Institutions and Alternatives, contends that, on any given day during the past year, 42% of the District's black men aged 18 through 35 could be found caught in some part of the criminal justice system, primarily because of police sweeps brought about by the drug trade.

About 70% of this group "are arrested by the time they turn 35" and over the course of their lives the figure rises to 85%. As one might expect, Miller argues that this situation spells disaster both for black men and the black community in the District of Columbia and, by further extension, the nation's civil society (De Parle, 1992). The policy of more and more arrests of drug dealers and users, coupled with mandatory sentencing procedures, is an utter failure.

The underclass is a surplus population and a colossal inconvenience to society as a whole. Those who know there are not enough prisons to hold them all are either pushing for more prisons, foolishly not realizing that once built they too will soon become overcrowded, or are content to let the underclass stew in their own juices. After all, who in their right mind would go for a stroll in America's impoverished inner cities? Yet who in their right mind would stroll through such places if all the narcotics available in them suddenly disappeared? Poor and despised people without drugs are still poor and despised. How they manage their wretched lives is more a miracle than a crime, even when they manage it through crime. Consider, too, the future when those currently imprisoned get out. Surely there are few intelligent people who still think that the experience of living in prison makes for better prepared citizens: more thoughtful and skillful, more humane and caring. In this human wasteland drugs play a large part as they increasingly provide reasons for living and dying.

America's drug policies are obtusely shortsighted. Twenty years ago the state of Virginia found that although more emphasis on drug enforcement in the larger cities and counties brought about more arrests, the state was failing "to stem, or even remain abreast of, the tide of drug abuse" (Virginia State Crime Commission, 1972). The solution in those days was to provide the police with an elaborate intelligence system, better data gathering, a reorientation of targets from street users to traffickers, more support for undercover activities, and an intelligent coordination of criminal justice. John E. Ingersoll, the Director of the Bureau of Narcotics and Dangerous Drugs, was quoted for support:

> The new horizons of drug enforcement require the strengthening of State Narcotic and Dangerous Drug enforcement capabilities as an aid to local law enforcement, and to provide the necessary mobility, undercover operations, drug abuse prevention co-

ordination, laboratory services, and training so sorely needed in most states. In some there is no one to carry out even the most rudimentary program and we urge the creation of such State Units.

These calls for more concentration, specialization, funding, technical support, and undercover work have been fulfilled, and they have failed. Those who still believe drug dealing and drug use are actually amenable to the endless proliferation of ever more sophisticated law enforcement are trapped in a kind of engineering mind-set that knows little about human craving.

The ambivalence of law enforcement is its most positive feature. At its worst, law enforcement is incurably vicious and ironically anti-American. The disappearing Fourth Amendment attests to this latter fact. Kenneth C. Haas (1990) reports that, increasingly, public employees, for whom there are no reasonable grounds to suspect drug use, nevertheless must urinate on command. Their specimens are then tested to determine if the urine contains drugs. Should the test be positive, the subject's career is in jeopardy. Aside from the many documented problems concerning the accuracy of such tests, they also are an unprecedented invasion of privacy. The inspection of employee's urine is an extension of state power through an erosion of the right against unwarranted search and seizure. There are now numerous exceptions to the increasingly archaic warrant requirement. Haas lists them while noting that they are considered by many to be far too few rather than too numerous: the exigent circumstances exception; the search incident to arrest exception; the stop-and-frisk exception; the consent exception; the automobile exception; the hot-pursuit exception; the plain-view exception; the open-fields exception; the abandoned-property exception; the misplaced-trust exception; the inventory-search exception; the border-search exception; the administrative-search exception; the school-search exception; and, finally, the private-citizen exception. Constitutionalists can yet take heart, though, as the "still breathing" exception is still to be decided.

Even though one of the major consequences of drug ferreting is alienation, there is some comfort in knowing that the production of alienation creates new forms of employment. There are more and more jobs in security and surveillance and a clearly pressing need for many urine- and hair-gatherers and testers. The manufacturing of drug testing machines and the development of testing procedures should help anxious young engineers and chemists searching for worthwhile careers. Developing drug user profiles, which generally succeed in making minorities vulnerable, keeps a generation of so-called social scientists working hard at the federal grant trough constructing questionnaires and crunching numbers in order to make these insightful profiles. Because minorities with money are *ipso facto* suspect, and scraggly whites acting nervously almost equally so, airport sleuths have their preventive work brilliantly and neatly laid out. Knowing this, however, it seems clear that scraggly whites and blacks with cash who wish to fly somewhere have plenty about which to be nervous. The circle of behavior and preventive policing is thus closed.

The invidious erosion of privacy is one product of drug enforcement zealotry. The deleterious impact on law enforcement is another. Enforcing drug laws places otherwise fairly decent men and women in constant peril from angry and threatened drug dealers, from the hazards of corruption and complicity, and from the danger of becoming brutalizing martinets. The Los Angeles Police Department's less than exemplary handling of Rodney King is instructive. Struck full force with police batons over fifty times (mostly while on the ground) and electrified with stunguns, the black man was bludgeoned into the hospital ostensibly for a traffic violation. The police officers' defense: "We thought he might have taken PCP and been real dangerous, and they don't feel hardly anything when they're high on PCP." Reasonable force, they say; afraid of PCP addicts, they say; prudent police action, they say. Of course some police officers like to beat blacks, and now, when caught in old-fashioned brutality, they have the drug panic at hand as an explanation.

Police corruption, when it comes to drug enforcement, is legendary. About a quarter of a century ago in New York an investigation into narcotics found police eager to be assigned to Harlem drug work in order to make extra money. Some used their political patrons to help them get transferred. In fact, the New York State Commission of Investigation (1972) reported that drug corruption had become an equal opportunity issue. Black politicians tried to intercede for black cops "certain that the black policemen were being discriminated against because they were not allowed to participate in the graft and corruption on the Narcotics Squad" that worked Harlem. Recurring scandals in the U.S. and elsewhere make it clear that policing narcotics has become the most criminogenic of occupations.

When drug dealers are caught, even police drug dealers, the corruption typically moves to another, even worse level. Portions of a letter written in January 1988 by a convicted cop in Miami highlights this. Addressed to a federal judge, a U.S. Attorney and a Florida State Attorney, the petitioner did not deny his guilt — "I was once a good cop who went bad and became a criminal and was hiding behind a police uniform and a badge" — but did want to alert the authorities to the condition of the Florida Bar. His attorneys, as well as those of his fellow defendants, demanded huge cash payments for services, advised how to avoid reporting illicit income, committed perjury, and hid witnesses. When his case moved from state to federal court he retained another attorney. This lawyer immediately demanded U.S.$125 000 in cash, wanted much more very soon thereafter, and then participated in a murder conspiracy to eliminate an unfriendly witness. Though this is an isolated case, it speaks to a far larger problem.

Sigmund Freud taught long ago that wit often masks hostility. Thus Americans' true feelings toward the Bar: "You're trapped in a room with a tiger, cobra, and a lawyer. You have a gun but only two bullets. What do you do? Shoot the lawyer twice, of course." The public's esteem for lawyers competes for "rock bottom" with that of the public's admiration for politicians. Perhaps the disgust with the former reinforces the contempt for the latter who are also mostly attorneys. Corruption, stupidity or a sullen craftiness, joined with a crushing selfishness, are what the public seems to see when it is forced to think of the Bar and, by extension, politicians.

This attitude, in fact, has long fueled the popularity of cop and private eye films. A good cop is one who disdains the morons he works with in the criminal justice system and simply shoots the bad guys. A good private eye is one who disdains all the imbeciles in the criminal justice system, including rogue cops, and simply shoots the bad guys. The plot engine in many of these films runs on the fuel of official corruption. To step out of ruminations about movies and TV, it appears that the police system, the legal system, the judiciary, and the prison system are generally held in revulsion.

But there is still more about the "war on drugs" that is far more troubling than anything mentioned previously. What if massive amounts of drugs have been provided to Americans by the U.S.

government itself? On the face of it, this is not an unreasonable proposition given what is already known about U.S. intelligence operations in Laos during the Vietnam War. Yet I mean to go beyond that to the real cocaine barons of the 1970s and 1980s. If the data I have collected are accurate then corruption is truly unbounded.

On March 11, 1980, a colonel in the U.S. military signed an astonishing affidavit. At the time he was the Commanding Officer of a Special Forces Group (Airborne). Under oath he stated that in December 1975 he was informed by another colonel about a classified mission inside Colombia called Operation Watch Tower. Two months later he commanded the second Operation Watch Tower mission under the direction of the Central Intelligence Agency. This mission lasted 22 days and its purpose "was to establish a series of three electronic beacon towers beginning outside Bogota, Columbia [sic] and running northeast to the border of Panama. Once the Watch Tower teams (Special Action Teams) were in place, the beacon was activated to emit a signal that aircraft could fix on and fly undetected from Bogota into Panama, landing at Albrook Air Station." During this mission, "30 high performance aircraft landed safely at Albrook where the planes were met by Colonel Tony Noriega, who is a Panama Defense Force Officer currently assigned to the Customs and Intelligence Section."

Point eight of the affidavit states: "The cargo flown from Columbia [sic] into Panama was cocaine." Also participating in Watch Tower was the "U.S. Army Southern Command in Panama." A third mission was performed the following month. This one included 40 aircraft and involved a firefight between the colonel's Special Action Team at Turbo, Colombia and around 40 to 50 Colombians. "Action intelligence reports identified the armed men as local bandits."

Just prior to the affidavit, the CIA head of operation informed the colonel that there were similar activities elsewhere in the world. Pakistan and the Golden Triangle were named. "In both areas of the world," he was informed, "the CIA and other intelligence agencies are using the illegal narcotics flow to support forces fighting to overthrow communist governments, or governments that are not friendly towards the United States." Money from the drug operations was laundered through a series of banks; "over 70% of the profits were laundered through the banks in Panama" while most of the rest went to Switzerland. A large amount of the money was "then used to purchase weapons to arm the various factions that the CIA saw as friendly towards the United States."

Those from the CIA involved in Watch Tower were soon involved in the Iran/Contra affair, according to a letter by another military officer attached to the National Security Council (NSC) and addressed to a well-known lieutenant colonel in Special Forces. These other officers were attempting to solve the Watch Tower puzzle, carrying on for the affidavit writer who was by that time dead, thought to have been murdered by an Israeli agent also deeply involved in Operation Watch Tower.

Although few have argued that narcotics had much to do with the Iran side of the Iran/Contra affair (perhaps wrongly, given that Pakistan was one of the backdoors for weapons to Iran and that Pakistan, with the aid and comfort of the U.S., concocted a booming heroin industry by 1980), many scholars and journalists have asserted otherwise for the Contra side. Indeed, Peter Dale Scott and Jonathan Marshall (1991) have established conclusively that the Contras trafficked in drugs under the aegis of U.S. authorities. But even the known role of Contra drug trafficking pales compared to what occurred in the formerly obscure state of Arkansas.

On November 27, 1987, an Arkansas State Police detective received a call from a reporter for information about an investigation into an aircraft maintenance firm named Rich Mountain Aviation. Located at a small airport in the little town of Mena, which stands virtually alone in the far west of Arkansas near the Oklahoma border, Rich Mountain was at the center of secret operations including cocaine smuggling in the name of national security. The reporter was seeking confirmation that the drug network operating out of Rich Mountain was part of Lt. Colonel Oliver North's network. He believed this group was smuggling cocaine into the U.S. through Mena and using the profits to support the Contras as well as themselves.

Arkansas State Police Detective Russell Welch properly told the reporter nothing because, in his mind, the investigation into drug smuggling at and through Mena by the Adler Berriman (Barry) Seal organization was still ongoing, even though Seal himself had been murdered the year before. Nonetheless, shortly after the reporter's call, Welch turned to his personal diary and expressed his growing despair over the course of events that blocked his way:

I feel like I live in Russia, waiting for the secret police to pounce down on me. The government has gotten out of control. Too many secret meetings, and secret meetings based on secret meetings. The falcon no longer answers the falconer. Nothing good can come from this. Men of no account find themselves in positions of power and suddenly crimes become legal. National Security!? A small group of men decide national security for the millions.

In the meantime all of us cops need to stay in our place. Arrest the street people and the poor people so that they will stay in their place and not bother those with power and money. Should a cop cross over the line and dare to investigate the rich and powerful he might well prepare himself to become the victim of his own government, the government of the United States of America.

The cops are all afraid to tell what they know for fear that they will lose their jobs or go to jail themselves.

As if in answer to his deepest suspicions, Welch was called by an Arkansas sheriff six weeks later who related that he had information indicating that U.S. Senator Robert Dole was concerned about the Rich Mountain investigation. In particular, the sheriff's informant stated that Dole was worried that the investigation might in some way harm George Bush.

And it might have, had it not been subverted. While Bush was Vice President he was deeply involved on the operational level of President Reagan's drug war. It was to Bush's staff that Barry Seal went when he needed immunity from prosecution. And it was Bush's staff that sent him to Florida to cut a deal with Drug Enforcement Administration (DEA) officials there. Seal negotiated an immunity deal with the DEA in Miami on March 24, 1984, that left him free from prosecution for any activities beginning after that date. (The Arkansas investigators concentrated on Seal's criminal activities during the period from April 1982 until the grant of immunity.) It was this same staff that was supposedly in charge of the Mena operation, in particular Don Gregg, later named Ambassador to South Korea by President Bush. And now it must be added that Bush was said to be at least knowledgeable about Operation Watch Tower in the colonel's affidavit discussed earlier. In fact, Bush was CIA Director when the nefarious operation was hatched.

Welch's comrade-in-arms in the smuggling investigation, which officially began in 1985, was William C. Duncan, then a Special Agent with the Criminal Investigation Division of the Internal Revenue

Service (IRS) assigned to Fayetville, Arkansas. Duncan was a law enforcement over-achiever, a true believer in his organization's virtue. But over the course of the following years he, like Welch, would face a similar profound disillusionment. Duncan's, however, was fashioned first from the actions of corrupt IRS officers who appear to have done everything possible to prevent him from moving forward with his end of the investigation into the Mena drug smuggling network, money laundering by and through Rich Mountain Aviation.

He was ordered by IRS Disclosure Litigation attorneys to perjure himself before the U.S. House of Representatives Subcommittee on Crime. The Subcommittee, which had subpoenaed Duncan to testify at a hearing in February 1988, was seeking general information about the Barry Seal smuggling enterprise at Mena, Arkansas, and particular intelligence passed to Duncan by a Seal confederate alleging knowledge of a $400 000 bribe of U.S. Attorney General Edwin Meese. The IRS attorneys directed Duncan to deny any knowledge of this. He refused to commit perjury and thus began Duncan's subsequent hard fall.

Harassed by his superiors in the IRS over the course of the next few years, Duncan finally resigned. Brief employment with the Subcommittee on Crime came next. He was hired as an investigator, supposedly to continue working on the Arkansas matter. But the Subcommittee's actual support for this work was at best lukewarm, a far cry from its publicly stated hard-line stance. Duncan, though, took it quite seriously and this was more than enough for unknown enemies to continue their pressure on him. The most damaging move against him came within the Capitol itself. Though licensed to carry a weapon and protected by congressional precedent and case law, Duncan was illegally jailed by the Capitol police for possessing a firearm. During this ordeal he was handcuffed to a wall nearly six hours at District of Columbia police headquarters. After this odd and cruel episode, which was ultimately protested by the Subcommittee and marked by footdragging on the part of the U.S. Attorney who unsuccessfully pressured him to plead guilty to a misdemeanor, Duncan left his shaky Washington haven. Eventually he found employment with the Arkansas Attorney General's Office in the Medicaid Fraud Division.

Duncan was pushed to the edge by the disintegration of his lawman's faith. In testimony before the Subcommittee on Commerce,

Consumer, and Monetary Affairs, he stated that "feelings of rage, disgust and helplessness" were constant as he discovered "he was powerless to deal with managers within IRS who perceived me as a troublemaker, and even a traitor, because I insisted on telling the truth." Duncan suppressed his anger on joining the Arkansas Attorney General's staff. But even then, he reported to the Subcommittee, the harassment continued. The U.S. Attorney for the Western District of Arkansas informed the Arkansas Attorney General that he would not prosecute any medicaid fraud cases brought by Duncan. This judicial officer was the one who had deliberately mishandled the hard evidence on drug smuggling, perjury, and money laundering gathered by Duncan and Welch from 1985 through 1987. No indictments were ever returned.

"Why did this happen? What could have been important enough for the Department of Justice and the Department of the Treasury to join hands in an effort which resulted in such interference?" Duncan asked rhetorically in his statement before the House Subcommittee on Commerce, Consumer, and Monetary Affairs. He answered his own questions:

> . . . during the period 1984 through 1986, the Mena, Arkansas Airport was an important hub/waypoint for transshipment of drugs, weapons and Central American "Contra" and Panamanian Defense Force personnel who were receiving covert training in a variety of specialties in the Nella community, located ten miles north of the Mena, Arkansas Airport. The evidence details a bizarre mixture of drug smuggling, gun running, money laundering and covert operations by Barry Seal, his associates, and both employees and contract operatives of the United States Intelligence Services. The testimony reveals a scheme whereby massive amounts of cocaine were smuggled into the State of Arkansas, and profits were partially used to fund covert operations. (House of Representatives, 1991)

Duncan and Welch were not aware then that they had in their grasp the potential "smoking gun" of the Contra affair. National security agents working for the White House meshed their operations with the drug- and gun-running activities of Barry Seal, and then continued with elements of Seal's organization after his murder in 1986. Though Seal's activities have been closely scrutinized by other writers, all have missed his move to Arkansas, and thus the ties binding Seal to the North network.

That is not to say that Seal's work as a DEA informer guided by Miami agents, and his subsequent attempt under CIA and NSC direction to prove that Colombia's cocaine giants, Pablo Escobar and Jorge Ochoa, had shifted part of their operation to Nicaragua, are not well known. They were the subject of congressional hearings, testimony before President Reagan's Commission on Organized Crime, and were reported on in both the print media and several books. But none of the writers or investigators realized that Seal had been a CIA asset since the early 1970s and had either relocated his smuggling headquarters to Arkansas in the early 1980s or had at least opened a thriving new branch there.

Seal had been first arrested in Louisiana on arms smuggling charges in 1972 when he was a TWA pilot. Other members of this conspiracy included organized crime figures and a prominent Texas banker. The case was allowed to languish until it was finally dropped on grounds of national security. Not much was heard about Seal until around 1977 when Louisiana law enforcement became aware that he had become a major smuggler. His headquarters were then in Baton Rouge. From that point on, Seal and Louisiana State Police officers played cat-and-mouse. Determined to end Seal's operations, either to jail him or convince him to inform, State Police officers braced Seal one day saying that either he would "flip" or sooner or later they would have evidence sufficient to shut him down permanently. Seal refused the offer and countered with his own. "How about," he asked, "if I leave the state?" The lawmen were not interested.

In an attempt to evade Louisiana authorities, and perhaps on the advice of his intelligence controls, Seal eventually expanded operations to Arkansas. Interestingly enough, Seal's move followed that of Raymond Varnado, a convicted arms smuggler from Louisiana, who was imprisoned in Texarkana until 1979. Upon his release, Varnado relocated to Nella, Arkansas, a wilderness section approximately ten miles north of Mena. There he worked with U.S. intelligence officers in what reportedly became a hidden training center for Latin American gunmen and covert operatives including select members of the Panamanian Defense Forces. A year or so later, Barry Seal was in Mena.

Everything that went on in Mena and Nella, and in other towns in Arkansas that played a role in the drugs and weapons saga, is still not known. There are almost monthly surprises. For example, in winter of 1991-92, Arkansas Congressman Bill Alexander had his chief of staff draft a synopsis of the Mena investigation. In this account the Mena airport was found to be "a training site for Contra pilots along with elements of the PLO and Panamanian Defense Forces." This was in addition to its use in the guns-for-drugs smuggling "tied to the Contra supply operation." Furthermore, the report suggests the DEA was fully aware that Seal was permitted by other U.S. government elements "to smuggle drugs back into the country." Alexander also charges that one of the band of pilots who worked with Seal at Mena/Nella claims to have been introduced to the rotund smuggler in 1983 by "Lt. Colonel Oliver North."

Congressman Alexander knows a great deal about what took place in Mena. But neither he nor anyone else knows the full story. Alexander, therefore, has called numerous times for a full and open investigation. He even squeezed US$25 000 out of a House appropriations bill a couple of years ago that was intended to support Duncan in a last ditch attempt to close the book on Mena. From Alexander the ball went to Arkansas Attorney General Winston Bryant who had campaigned for the office pledging to "get to the bottom of Mena." Eventually Bryant passed the ball to Governor Bill Clinton. On February 18, 1992, Bryant requested the Governor to "authorize the creation of a position for a special investigator assigned to the Arkansas State Police to compile evidence related to allegations of drug smuggling at the Mena airport during the early to mid 1980s." Concurrently a second letter was sent by Bryant to Colonel Tommy Goodwin of the Arkansas State Police informing him that Duncan "will be detached from this agency to serve as a temporary special investigator attached to the Arkansas State Police." Following this, Duncan was ordered by the Attorney General to "lay off" Mena while in his office.

By April of 1992 nothing further in this matter had been accomplished. The money so arduously obtained by Congressman Alexander long ago rests somewhere in the nether world of Arkansas politics and Duncan sits forlornly wondering when the next shoe will drop.

Checkmate.

References

Bartlett, Sarah. 1992." New York Logs 500 000 Jobs Lost Since 1989, a Record High." *New York Times.* April 16. B1.

DeParle, Jason. 1992. "Young Black Men in Capital: Study Finds 42% in Courts." *New York Times.* April 18. 1.

Draper, Theodore. 1991. *A Very Thin Line.* New York: Hill and Wang.

Epstein, Jason. 1992. "The Tragical History of New York." *New York Review of Books.* April 9. 45-52.

Haas, Kenneth C. 1990. "The Supreme Court Enters the 'Jars Wars': Drug Testing, Public Employees, and the Fourth Amendment." *Dickinson Law Review* 94: 305-371.

House of Representatives. 1991. "William C. Duncan Testimony (July 24, 1991) Before Committee on Government Operations, Subcommittee on Commerce, Consumer, and Monetary Affairs," *Continued Investigation of Senior Level Employee Misconduct and Mismangement at the IRS: Hearings.* Washington. D.C.: U.S. Government Printing Office.

New York State Commission of Investigation. 1972. *Narcotics Law Enforcement in New York City: A Report.*

Scott, Peter Dale and Jonathan Marshall. 1991. *Cocaine Politics: Drugs, Armies, and the CIA in Central America.* Los Angeles and Berkley, CA: University of California Press.

Virginia State Crime Commission. 1972. *Report of the Organized Crime Detection Task Force.* Richmond, Virginia.

Introduction —————————

Mark S. Gaylord and Harold H. Traver

The essays contained in *Drugs, Law and the State* are based on the notion that drug control policy largely reflects the society in which it is found. This idea, of course, derives from the traditional sociological position that the substantive content of law depends primarily on the larger society. For the most part this idea is substantiated in these essays, but the reader will also learn that smaller nations are currently under pressure from larger and more powerful countries to adopt drug control policies that run counter to their national traditions. Yet here, too, the idea that public policy reflects social organization helps explain why some countries (for example, the United States) attempt to exert pressure on others to harmonize their drug control policy, while other countries (for example, the Netherlands and Denmark) strenuously resist such pressure.

Taken as a whole, the essays in this collection assume that modern drug control policies are explained best by theories that emphasize the role of ideology, legitimacy, and history. While this idea is neither novel nor especially profound, it does have the merit of directing attention to research questions less often addressed by traditional criminology. For example, whereas conventional criminologists might ask why some people use illegal drugs and others do not, a number of our contributors ask why drug use is defined as crime. Moreover, a number of essays in this book examine how historical forces have shaped drug control policy in certain societies, while others, conversely, ask how drug control policies have affected the societies that spawned them.

These essays were prepared for a conference on crime, drugs, and social control that was held at the Department of Sociology of the University of Hong Kong in December 1988. The conference was organized under the auspices of the Research Committee for the Sociology of Deviance and Social Control (International Sociological Association) in association with the Hong Kong Society of Criminology. The participants, representing countries from Europe, North America, Asia, and Africa, met for three days to present papers and to discuss general issues involved in comparative research on public policy. Notwithstanding the diversity of societies and cultures that were represented by the participants, the conference theme — crime, drugs and social control — provided a coherent focus for our collaborative efforts.

The nine essays contained here fall into three distinct groups. In Part One, "Drug Control Policy and the State," four papers examine drug control policy in relation to the interests of the state as a defined interest group. In Denmark, Spain, and Finland we find three relatively small countries whose recent history of drug control policy offers insights not readily available from the study of larger, more frequently studied, nations.

In "The Consequences of Prohibition: Crime, Corruption, and International Narcotics Control," William J. Chambliss argues that, though anti-alcohol laws were abolished in the early 1930s, the prohibition era never actually ended, whether in the U.S. or elsewhere. While one form of drug, alcohol, had become legalized, others, particularly cocaine, heroin, and marijuana, were either criminalized or subjected to renewed law enforcement as previously dormant laws became reactivated. As a consequence, all the ills and problems created by alcohol prohibition were institutionalized. International cartels emerged and grew rich and powerful, while fine-tuning their enterprises. The economies of entire nation-states became dependent on the production, export, and distribution of illicit drugs, and law enforcement and other officials were corrupted. As demand for illicit drugs spiralled to unimagined heights, profits have soared to such levels that today the gross volume of business in illicit drugs makes it one of the most important industries in the world. While mindful that an ideal solution is illusory, Chambliss offers alternative social policies that promise greater benefits and fewer costs than prohibition.

In "Drugs and Social Control in Scandinavia: A Case Study in International Moral Entrepreneurship," Jørgen Jepsen examines drug control policy in Scandinavia, a seemingly homogeneous region not yet fully integrated with Europe. Specifically, he reveals that Scandinavia's homogeneity is more apparent than real, as striking differences exist between Denmark (Jepsen's home) and Norway, Sweden, and Finland. His specific contribution is to demonstrate how these differences reflect historic national traditions (and divisions) within Scandinavia. Beyond this, Jepsen calls for increased mutual respect and tolerance among nations that, for obvious historical reasons, cannot possibly hope to always agree on public policy. In the face of intense international pressure for Denmark and other relatively small countries to adopt increasingly repressive drug control policies, Jepsen cautions against confusing the call for international co-operation with moral imperialism.

Axel R. Reeg, in "Drugs and the Law in Post-Franco Spain," examines the changes in Spanish society and drug control policy in the 17 years since the death of the dictator, General Franco. This period has ushered in a degree of liberalization that would have been unthinkable during Franco's time. But along with rapid economic growth and new political freedoms, Spain has also experienced increased drug use. Reeg documents the changes, both major and minor, in Spanish drug control policy throughout these years. In his view, Spain's more recent attempts to control drug use have made a bad situation even worse. In a section that demonstrates how Europe's historical and cultural diversity has given rise to different views on how to respond to increased drug use, Reeg describes how informed opinion among specialists in the field of drug control policy has gradually moved towards increased liberalization, if not yet outright legalization, of drug use in Spain.

In "Finnish Drug Control Policy: Change and Accommodation," Ahti Laitinen expands further the theme originating with Jørgen Jepsen: that increasing global interdependence disadvantages smaller countries that desire to maintain public policies in conformance with their history and cultural traditions. In Finland, Laitinen describes a country more similar to Norway and Sweden than to Denmark in its cultural conservatism, yet set apart from its Nordic neighbors both linguistically and in terms of its isolationist foreign policy. In an important section called "Drug Policy in the Nordic Countries,"

Laitinen observes that Finland's alcohol control policy is becoming more liberal in response to pressures to conform with European-wide policies, while at the same time its drug control policies are likely to become more punitive for the same reason.

In Part Two, "The Political Economy of Drugs," four papers examine the political-economic nexus of the drug trade (smuggling, trafficking, money laundering, and organized crime), primarily in Asia. In the case of Hong Kong, Britain's opium trade with China in the nineteenth century constituted the colony's *raison d'etre*. While such is not the case today, Hong Kong continues to serve as a conduit for Golden Triangle heroin to Europe, North America and Australia, and, more importantly, as a financial laundry for the ill-gotten gains of both local and foreign drug trafficking organizations.

In "The Chinese Laundry: International Drug Trafficking and Hong Kong's Banking Industry," Mark S. Gaylord examines Britain's last remaining colony in Asia, reputed to be one of the world's leading centers for the laundering of drug money. Located on the southeast coast of China, Hong Kong is not far from the Golden Triangle in Burma, Laos and Thailand, the source of much of the world's heroin supply. Ethnic Chinese criminal organizations based in Hong Kong and elsewhere have long been involved in the refining, transporting and financing of Southeast Asian heroin. With its bank secrecy laws, its large and sophisticated international banking industry, and its complete absence of currency exchange controls, Gaylord demonstrates that Hong Kong has all of the necessary components of a modern financial secrecy jurisdiction. While government spokesmen adamantly deny the allegations, compelling evidence exists to support the claim that billions of dollars are being washed annually in Hong Kong by both local and overseas drug traffickers, eventually to be reinvested throughout the world.

Masayuki Tamura's paper, "The Yakuza and Amphetamine Abuse in Japan," examines the organization of drug trafficking in Japan, focusing on the monopolistic control of amphetamine importation and distribution by the several large, nationwide crime syndicates that are collectively referred to as the Yakuza. While mindful of the longstanding and intimate connections between the Yakuza and nationalistic, right-wing Japanese politicians, Tamura focuses principally on the history of drug use in Japan, the organization of stimulant distribution throughout the country, and the likelihood of increased use of other illegal drugs (for example, cocaine) among the Japanese.

In "The Organized Crime/Drug Connection: National and International Perspectives," Ernesto Ugo Savona situates drug trafficking within the larger context of organized crime. He argues that drug trafficking has become an international concern because organized crime itself has become increasingly international in character. Through a complex chain of cause and effect, social control has by necessity become increasingly global in order to contain international criminal organizations whose activities increasingly include, but are not restricted to, the production, transportation and distribution of illegal drugs throughout the world.

Harold H. Traver, in "Colonial Relations and Opium Control Policy in Hong Kong, 1841-1945," tells the story of how, under British rule, Hong Kong's colonial government developed an increasingly strong fiscal dependence on revenue from the retail sale of opium within the colony itself, a dependence that began soon after the colony's founding and continued well into the twentieth century. Yet, ironically, since 1945, Hong Kong has adopted an increasingly punitive stance to drug trafficking, to the point that its legal strictures are now among the harshest in the world. In his essay, Traver asks the pertinent question: How did the definition of the problem change from one of how to secure and protect an important source of government revenue to one of how to suppress domestic drug use?

In Part Three, "Future Directions," John F. Galliher's essay, "Illegal Drugs: Where We Stand and What We Can Do," examines the current status of drug control policy in the United States, and finds it sorely in need of change. He describes how current policy, far from being the product of rational analysis, is largely the legacy of fear, ignorance, and racism. In its place, he proposes a methodology for gradually reducing existing penalties while simultaneously increasing federal funding for public education and medical treatment. These measures would be monitored by a rigorous evaluation program to detect changes in use patterns. Such a methodology might indicate that gradual decriminalization can lead safely to eventual legalization, but the advantage of such a program, Galliher argues, is that all the answers need not be known before alternatives are tried.

The authors of the following essays are well aware that they have not written the final word on drugs, law, and the state. However, they are convinced that this topic is important and should be pursued. As editors, we have been instructed and inspired by our contributors' often fresh and original insights. Many of their ideas stand in marked contrast to conventional thinking on drug control policy. It is our hope that we can continue to learn together.

Given current definitions, it is easy to forget that, less than one hundred years ago, Western governments defined the international drug trade as legitimate business, and imposed this view on the rest of the world. Throughout those years opium was the principal commodity, although morphine, cannabis and, later, heroin and cocaine were also important. Various forms of medicinal opium and opium derivatives were widely sold and used in the West, while raw and prepared (smoking) opium were important items of commerce in the East. The Asian opium trade fueled European colonial expansion in the Far East, provided the financial basis for Britain's rule of India, and created vast personal fortunes. The law protected, rather than proscribed, the opium trade. Laws prohibited the sale and consumption of opium, but only in its contraband form, and, when deemed necessary by the European powers, restricted the sale of competing drugs such as morphine, heroin, and cocaine on the grounds that they were a public danger.

Throughout the nineteenth century, the Asian opium trade was carefully nurtured and controlled by an alliance of colonial governments, international trading firms and local entrepreneurs who competed for government franchises for the importation and sale of opium. For many decades the opium trade was one of the largest and most vibrant examples of free enterprise in the world. Opium was not only a source of huge profits, it served also to maintain a cheap and compliant Asian labor force by lessening the psychological and physical pains associated with harsh and exploitative working conditions. By the second half of the nineteenth century, the European colonial powers clearly had become economically drug dependent.

Eventually, however, the opium trade's success sowed the seeds for its destruction. From the very beginning, grave reservations were expressed about the morality of the opium trade. As early as 1840 a debate in the British House of Commons heard opium condemned as an "infamous contraband traffic" (Collis, 1964:267-286; Lewis, 1910:21-22). As the trade gathered momentum in the latter half of the nineteenth century so did calls for its abolition. In 1891 the Anglo-Oriental Society for the Suppression of the Opium Trade promoted a major, though inconclusive, parliamentary inquiry into the opium trade. Within China itself, discontent flaired up sporadically in opposition to the sale and consumption of opium. However, no effective steps were taken either in Britain or China to suppress its continuance. On the British side, it was postulated that the loss of revenue would "render the Government of India insolvent" and that abolition "could not be considered within the scope of practical politics" (British Parliamentary Papers, 1971:431). On the Chinese side, a decision to legalize the opium trade in 1858 meant that it became a major producer, and, as with the European colonial powers, opium became the financial mainstay of the government (Endacott, 1973:272-273). Moreover, the European powers could rightly claim that given China's inability or unwillingness to control its own production, they themselves were under no obligation to control the drug's importation.

If not for the involvement of the United States in China and the Far East, it was possible that reservations over lost government revenue would have continued to take precedence over suppression. The United States' colonization of the Philippines and its growing involvement in the Chinese market had placed it in a position of direct competition with the established European powers for political and economic influence in East Asia. America's promotion of the "open door policy" and "dollar diplomacy" during this period was designed ostensibly to support the principles of Chinese territorial integrity and free trade, but their real purpose was to undercut European power in China. However, the lack of public support and military power seriously hampered the United States' ability to carry the fight directly to its European competitors.

The United States' status as a latecomer to the international power game had its advantages, nonetheless. While forced to play the unwanted role of a minor player in the opium trade, the United States was in a good position to attack one of the major financial pillars of colonial rule in Asia. As early as the Second Opium War (1856-58) the U. S. government had begun to disassociate itself from the trade. In 1880, in return for Chinese assurances that it would take steps to restrict emigration to the West, the United States signed a treaty with China prohibiting American merchants from trading opium or shipping it on American vessels. The Americans also took steps to suppress opium in the Philippines soon after they took control in 1898, and continued to condemn the opium trade in other parts of Asia. Thus, by the end of the century, the Americans, in contrast to the Europeans, had nothing to lose and everything to gain by occupying the high moral ground regarding the trafficking in opium. If the United States could not hope to win the power struggle going on in China it could at least sponsor a symbolic crusade that would, if successful, undermine the financial basis for European colonial rule in Asia.

The origins of America's symbolic crusade against the opium trade were not confined to its ambitions for international influence. Suppression was a vote-winning domestic political issue as well. The history of drug control laws in the United States has been closely linked with efforts to control minority groups, who have often been represented as the major users, and a desire to protect such "middle class values" as hard work and sobriety (Musto, 1973). There is also reason to believe that the United States has a history of extensive drug abuse. By 1924, for instance, federal authorities estimated there were over 200 000 opiate addicts in the United States (McCoy, 1972:5).

The suppression of opium was not in the immediate interests of either China or the European powers. In 1906 China was producing approximately 20 000 metric tons of opium and importing another 3300 metric tons (Foreign Office, 1929:14; Anti-Opium Association, 1922:16-17). At the same time, opium revenues continued to be the financial mainstay of European colonial governments in East Asia and India. However, following the Boxer Rebellion in 1900, a rising tide of nationalism, together with increasing international pressure largely orchestrated by the United States, resulted in China and Britain signing an agreement in 1907 in which Britain agreed to cease exporting opium from India to China over a ten-year period in return for which China would attempt to suppress its domestic production. For China, the loss of revenue would be offset by the lessening of foreign control, while the European powers would still be able to ship opium to their other colonies and to process opium into morphine and patent medicines for the growing international market.

The United States seized the diplomatic initiative when it proposed that an International Opium Commission be held in Shanghai in 1909 to consider the situation in regard to countries other than Britain that might produce and export opium to China. Later that same year, the United States issued invitations to those governments attending the Shanghai Commission to attend another meeting at The Hague to draw up what would be the first opium convention. At their meeting, the major European powers and the United States agreed to the "gradual and effective suppression" of raw and prepared opium and to the enactment of "pharmacy laws or regulations to confine to medical and legitimate purposes the manufacture, sale, and use" of morphine, cocaine, heroin, and medicinal opium (LaMotte, 1924:189-191). The Hague Conference provided guidelines for the formation of national and international drug legislation and set the tone for much of what was to follow.

Throughout the 1920s and 1930s the United States continued to promote what were known as the "American principles" of complete suppression of opium smoking, and the restriction of opium production to medicinal purposes only. Colonial governments were forced to adopt policies in support of opium suppression if they hoped to retain any legitimacy. At the same time, these new international agreements and the laws that accompanied them directly contradicted other state interests, in particular the need for a reliable and potent source of revenue. Whereas Europe's Far Eastern colonies previously had adopted a *laissez-faire* attitude that discouraged direct involvement in the sale of opium, the provisions of the Hague Convention and American pressure unintentionally encouraged direct government involvement as a means of controlling consumption. Given the enormous sums involved, it was difficult for officials to resist the temptation to neglect control efforts and to view government opium monopolies simply as a means of enhancing revenue. As a result, Europe's Far Eastern colonies became increasingly willing to engage in whatever subterfuge and pretext was necessary to protect a valuable source of revenue from international criticism.

Given the reluctance of colonial governments to break their dependence on opium revenues, it is not surprising that complete suppression continued to elude the United States until 1943, when it became strong enough to announce unilaterally that it would close all European opium monopolies in Japanese occupied territories as soon as they could be re-occupied by American forces. The privileges and concessions gained by the European powers in China also ended then for the same reasons. By the 1940s, the European powers were in no position to resist American demands, and America's symbolic crusade against opium ended successfully on the war's coattails.

America's response to the legislative requirements of the Hague Convention was the Harrison Act of 1914. This law required the registration of all legitimate drug companies and placed severe restrictions on the distribution of opium-based drugs. Although the Harrison Act was never intended to interfere with the legitimate right of physicians to treat their patients, a vague clause in the Act was interpreted by federal authorities to define drug addiction as something other than a medical problem. Goode (1984:109) estimates that by the mid-1920s, 25 000 physicians had been arrested and 3000 were serving jail sentences for prescribing prohibited drugs to their patients. As a result of the Harrison Act physicians ceased to treat addicts, and the addict was soon seen by the general public as a criminal and moral degenerate.

British drug laws of this period also reflected international opinion. As in the United States, Britain's Dangerous Drug Act of 1920 was framed along the lines laid down by the Hague Conference. Unlike the United States, though, Britain in the 1920s was ethnically homogeneous and virtually free of drug abuse. Consequently, the Dangerous Drug Act did not attempt to control putative dangerous minority groups. British authorities defined drug addiction as a medical problem and permitted doctors therefore to prescribe drugs as part of their treatment for addiction. Since the 1920s, Britain's drug laws have been tightened and the authority of doctors to prescribe drugs restricted, but the basic principle of medicalization has remained unchanged despite the dramatic rise in the rate of addiction.

The Japanese response to opium provides an interesting counterpoint to that of the United States and Britain during this period. Whereas the United States criminalized, and the British medicalized, the Japanese merchandised drugs. Early on, Japan had shown an acute awareness of the dangers posed by the opium trade and had instituted severe restrictions on the importation and sale of opium and opium derivatives. However, when faced with the problem of how to gain influence in China when Japan itself was still so poor, it chose to follow the example of the European colonial powers rather than join the United States in its symbolic crusade against opium. In fact, Japan improved on the European example by gaining control of the even more lucrative morphine and heroin trade. In 1916, the year before international restrictions were imposed, Britain exported nearly 25 000 kg of morphine to Japan. After 1916, Japan redirected its energies to become one of the world's largest producers of heroin. As late as 1927, a Dutch company managed to legally ship half the world's supply of heroin (3000 kg) to Japan (Foreign Office, 1929:30). Thus, in common with most of the European colonial powers, Japan publically supported the American principles of total suppression while privately pursuing what has been called the "most colossal and profitable monopoly in the world" (Foreign Office, 1921:40).

The elimination, in 1943, of government opium monopolies has had far-reaching consequences. Whereas previously the promotion of opium had gone hand in glove with the suppression of competing drugs, the elimination of government opium monopolies meant the loss of a powerful economic incentive for governments to engage in control efforts. Official commitment to the promotion and sale of opium enabled opium smoking to persist well into the twentieth century despite stiff competition from competing drugs such as morphine and heroin. But when the state withdrew from the opium trade, suppliers and consumers gravitated to heroin as a more cost effective drug (Westermeyer, 1976; Way, 1965).

Today, of course, drugs are being merchandised at a level unimaginable before World War II, but now the profits flow to criminal organizations rather than governments. World opinion, led by the United States, is arrayed generally in favor of hard-line measures, primarily directed at poor South American and Asian countries. The treatment of addiction as a medical problem, rather than moral or criminal, remains largely confined to a few European countries that have managed to resist America's insistence that drug suppression efforts be strengthened.

References

Anti-Opium Association. 1922. *The War Against Opium*. Tientsin: Tientsin Press Ltd.

British Parliamentary Papers. 1971. *China: Opium War and Opium Trade*. Vol. 31. Shannon: Irish University Press.

Collis, Maurice. 1964. *Foreign Mud*. London: Faber and Faber.

Endacott, George B. 1973. *A History of Hong Kong*, Rev. ed. Hong Kong: Oxford University Press.

Foreign Office. 1921. *Japan and the Morphia Trade*. Foreign Office Collection (F. O. 415), Part XVI, No. 32:40.

———. 1929. *Memorandum Respecting Opium in the Far East*. Foreign Office Collection (F. O. 415), Part XXVI, No. 6:11-43. Foreign Office Collection

415 was reprinted in 1974 as *The Opium Trade: 1910-1941*. Wilmington, DL: Scholarly Resources Inc.

Goode, Erich. 1984. *Deviant Behavior*, Second ed. Englewood Cliffs, NJ: Prentice-Hall.

LaMotte, Ellen. 1924. *The Ethics of Opium*. New York: Century Company.

Lewis, E. 1910. *Black Opium*. London: Marshall Brothers.

McCoy, Alfred. W. 1972. *The Politics of Heroin in Southeast Asia*. New York: Harper and Row.

Musto, David F. 1973. *The American Disease: Origins of Narcotic Control*. New Haven, CT: Yale University Press.

Way, E. L. 1965. "Control and Treatment of Drug Addiction in Hong Kong," pp 274-289, in *Narcotics*, edited by D. M. Wilner and G. G. Kassebaum. New York: McGraw-Hill.

Westermeyer, Joseph. 1976. "The Pro-Heroin Effects of Anti-Opium Laws in Asia." *Archives of General Psychiatry* 33:1135-1139.

Part I ━━━━━━━━━━

Drug Control Policy and the State

Part I

Drug Control Policy and
the State

1

The Consequences of Prohibition: Crime, Corruption, and International Narcotics Control

William J. Chambliss

Make no mistake about it, the prohibition era did not end in the United States or elsewhere in the world when the anti-alcohol laws were abolished in the early 1930s. The only change was that one form of drug, alcohol, was legalized, while other forms, particularly cocaine, heroin, and marijuana, were either criminalized or laws that were previously dormant suddenly took center stage in the law enforcement process (Lindesmith, 1969).

As a consequence, all of the ills and problems created by alcohol prohibition became institutionalized. International cartels engaged in smuggling illicit drugs emerged, grew wealthy and powerful, and fine-tuned their enterprises. The economies of nations throughout the world became dependent on the production, export, import, and distribution of drugs. Widespread corruption of law enforcement officials and legislators took place throughout the world. Nation-states spent billions of dollars with the left hand to suppress drug trafficking while encouraging it with the right hand. Demand for drugs increased worldwide as did supply. Profits rose to the point that today the gross volume of business in illicit drugs makes it one of the most important industries in the world.

Markets and Profits

The market in opium, heroin, cocaine, and marijuana in the United States generates a gross volume of business in excess of US$130 billion a year (Nadelmann, 1988). This makes the importation, sale, and distribution of illegal drugs an enterprise that generates more revenue than any of the largest multinational corporations in the world. It makes the gross volume of illegal drugs in the United States generate more capital than the gross national product of all but a dozen nations in the world. When the profits from illegal drugs in Europe and Asia are added to those from the United States, the importance of these economic enterprises to the world economy is enormous.

To suppose that law enforcement agencies can make even a slight dent in the operations of the thousands of well-established, firmly entrenched businesses spanning the economies of countries all over the world and employing hundreds of thousands of people from peasant farmers to heads of state is sheer folly.

Entire nation-states — Turkey, Colombia, Peru, Bolivia, Afghanistan — depend upon the production of drugs for their economic survival. Other nations, including the United States, Honduras, Panama, Burma, Thailand, Laos, Mexico, and even tiny Surinam, are so deeply enmeshed economically in the production and distribution of drugs that their economies would be severely affected and the existing political systems undermined were the "war on drugs" to be even moderately effective.

The impact of a successful "war on drugs" for the United States would be devastating. California is the largest agricultural producer in the United States, and the single largest cash crop of the state is marijuana. The United States pharmaceutical industry manufactures billions of amphetamines, barbiturates and assorted varieties of uppers and downers that are sold and distributed to the illegal drug market (Graham, 1972). The profits from these illegal sales are a bedrock of the profitability of the entire pharmaceutical industry.

In the last ten years, the United States has doubled its expenditure on law enforcement and the number of law enforcement officers at the state and local level. A significant portion of the effort of law enforcement agencies at all levels is an attempt to "stem the flow of drugs." No more evidence of the impossibility of affecting the illegal drug business through law enforcement need be cited than the fact that after 40 years of concerted effort, and the infusion of billions of dollars to increase the effectiveness of law enforcement efforts, the percentage of illegal drugs interdicted by U.S. law enforcement agencies remains at 10% of the total imported every year.

In the last 12 years, the number of people in America's prisons has doubled with the consequence that the United States now incarcerates a larger percentage of its population than any country in the world. Nearly 50% of the people in prison today are there for either the possession or sale of narcotics. Moreover, possession convictions account for more than 50% of those convicted on drug charges.

The ineffectiveness of these programs and expenditures is easy to see. Heroin, cocaine, crack, marijuana, and hashish are as readily available on the streets today as they were 30 years ago. Most users are middle-class white males; most people arrested are poor black males. There is more drug use on university campuses than in the ghetto, but it is the ghetto resident who is arrested and sentenced to prison. One in four black men between the ages of 18 and 27 is at this very moment either in jail, prison, on probation, or on parole — over half of them for drug offenses (Maurer, 1991).

The consequences of the "war on drugs" that so captures the imagination and rhetoric of politicians are human misery caused by the spread of diseases such as AIDS and hepatitis, the rampant rise in prostitution and crime in order to pay for the excessively priced drugs, the corruption of political and law enforcement officials, the creation of an uncontrolled and uncontrollable underground economy, and the institutionalization of crime at all levels in conjunction with the illegal drug markets.

One case in point should be sufficient to force a shift in the way we deal with drugs: the complicity of the largest, most powerful intelligence agency in the world in illegal drug trafficking. However, to understand this we must first understand that the *sine qua non* of the illegal drug trade is the art of smuggling.

Smuggling

During the era of alcohol prohibition, enterprising capitalists, labeled variously as "rumrunners" and bootleggers," created a whole new industry based on smuggling. Alcohol produced in Scotland, Cuba,

Canada, and a number of other countries was systematically smuggled into the United States, England, the Scandinavian countries, and other nations where alcohol sale was illegal. These entrepreneurs were brilliant in their business acumen. They purchased ships, licensed them, covered their cargoes of alcohol with spurious bills of lading, hired ship captains and transported the goods. The ships carrying the contraband anchored offshore and out of the reach of customs officials. Small boats plied the waters on moonless nights and ferried the cases of scotch and rum to the shore. Customs officials, even those who might have attempted to intercede in the traffic, were left wondering where to search out the faster, more agile boats capable of running up small rivers or crossing large bodies of water in short periods of time.

Not that the customs officials were a serious threat to the smugglers. Generous bribes were paid from the vast profits being made; bribes which in any case were lower than the taxes that would be paid by the same people once alcohol became legal.

Once alcohol became legalized, the smugglers scarcely took time to catch their breath before they were loading their ships with opium and heroin, drugs for which there was less demand than alcohol but for which a market existed. Indeed, in the ensuing 50 years the market would prove to be more manageable, more susceptible to the creation of monopolies, and vastly more profitable than illegal alcohol. Nevertheless, strategies had to change: airplanes replaced ships, and drugs could be buried in shipments of lumber, furniture, or automobile tires. But the principles were the same: government officials were bribed, pilots were hired and "legitimate" businessmen were co-opted into assisting in the shipment.

As in the days of the notorious Al Capone and Dutch Schultz, however, the government's franchise on violence was undermined. Smugglers could not protect their sources, their markets or their distribution networks through international contracts respected by international agreements. They therefore created their own legal system. Those who failed to pay for a shipment were taught a lesson. Kneecaps were drilled, innocent family members maimed and, if necessary, debtors were found in the trunks of cars or beneath six feet of water with concrete "shoes." The message was not lost on those who agreed to pay for a shipment of opium but yet failed to do so.

The smuggling of drugs became one of the most important enterprises to be firmly entrenched in the international system of trade. By the middle of the twentieth century, the profits from international narcotics smuggling would affect not only the nations that produced the basic resources of opium, heroin, hashish, and marijuana, it would also affect as well the importing nations and the very fabric of their governments.

The CIA in Vietnam

During the Vietnam War the U.S. Central Intelligence Agency became a partner in the smuggling of opium in Southeast Asia (McCoy, 1972; Chambliss, 1977). The U.S. inherited this practice from the French who, from the early days of colonialism in Indo-China, depended on the profits from opium to support the colonial government and later to insure the support of the opium producing hill tribes and to help finance the war against the communists (McCoy, 1972:27). Because of their proximity to the Chinese border, both France and the United States depended on the military support of the hill tribes in Cambodia, Laos, Thailand, and Vietnam. That support, in turn, required that the French and U.S. intelligence services cooperate with the production and distribution of opium, the hill tribes' only cash crop. Air America, the CIA airline in Vietnam, regularly transported bundles of opium from air strips in Laos, Cambodia, and Burma to Saigon and Hong Kong (Chambliss, 1977:56). An American stationed at Long Cheng, the secret Central Intelligence Agency military base in Northern Laos during the war, observed:

> . . . so long as the Meo leadership could keep their wards in the boondocks fighting and dying in the name of, for these unfortunates anyway, some nebulous cause . . . the Meo leadership [was paid off] in the form of a carte blanche to exploit U.S.-supplied airplanes and communications gear to the end of greatly streamlining the opium operations . . . (Chambliss, 1977:56)

Laotian Army General Ouane Rattikone told the author, in an interview in 1974, that he was the principal overseer of the shipment of opium out of the Golden Triangle via Air America. At the CIA base in Long Cheng were a number of military officers whose careers in state-organized crime continued after Vietnam: General Richard Secord, Thomas Clines, Theodore Schackley, and Michael Hand.

U.S. law did not permit the CIA or any of its agents to engage in the smuggling of opium. The agency officially denied involvement even in the face of overwhelming evidence of its involvement. Thus the U.S. was implicated in the perpetuation of a form of state-organized crime that, ironically, was responsible for the addiction and death of many of its own military. The necessity to curtail competition through violence, which characterizes the smuggling of opium, also implicated the United States in murder and assassination as different groups competed for control of the profits and territory.

When France withdrew from Vietnam and left the protection of democracy to the United States, the French intelligence service that preceded the CIA in managing the opium smuggling in Asia continued to support part of its clandestine operations through drug trafficking (Kruger, 1979). While these operations are shrouded in secrecy, the evidence is very strong that French intelligence forces helped to organize the movement of opium through the Middle East (especially Morocco) after their source of revenue from opium from Southeast Asia was cut off.

In 1969, Michael Hand, one of the agents stationed at Long Cheng during the time when Air America was shipping opium, moved to Australia, ostensibly as a private citizen. On arriving in Australia, he entered into a business partnership with an Australian national, Frank Nugan. In 1976 they established the Nugan Hand Bank in Sydney (New South Wales, 1982, 1983; Nihill, 1982). The Nugan Hand Bank began as a storefront operation with minimal investment of capital but almost immediately boasted deposits of over US$25 million. This rapid growth of the bank resulted from large deposits of secret funds, including funds from the CIA, belonging to narcotics and arms smugglers.

In addition to records from the Nugan Hand Bank that suggest the CIA used the bank as a conduit for its funds, the bank's connection to the CIA and other U.S. intelligence agencies is evidenced by the people who became directors and principal officers of the bank:

- Admiral Earl F. Yates, President of Nugan Hand Bank, former Chief of Staff for Strategic Planning of U.S. Forces in Asia and the Pacific during the Vietnam war.
- General Edwin F. Black, head of Nugan Hand Bank's Hawaii branch, commander of U.S. troops in Thailand during the Vietnam war, and later Assistant Army Chief of Staff for the Pacific.
- General Earle Cooke, Jr., head of Nugan Hand Bank's Washington office.

- George Farris, of Nugan Hand Bank's Hong Kong and Washington, D.C. offices, a former military intelligence specialist who had worked at a Special Forces training base in the Pacific.
- Bernie Houghton, Nugan Hand Bank's representative in Saudi Arabia, a former U.S. Naval Intelligence undercover agent.
- Thomas Clines, a Nugan Hand Bank operative who had helped arrange the takeover of a London-based bank and was former Director of Training in the CIA's Clandestine Service.
- Dale Holmgreen, board member and head of Nugan Hand Bank's Taiwan office, former Flight Service Manager in Vietnam for Civil Air Transport (the forerunner of Air America).
- General Roy Manor, head of Nugan Hand Bank's Philippine office, who later helped co-ordinate the aborted attempt to rescue the hostages held at the U.S. Embassy in Iran, former Chief of Staff for the U.S. Pacific Command and the U.S. government's liaison officer to Ferdinand Marcos, former President of the Philippines.

On the board of directors of the parent company that preceded the Nugan Hand Bank were Grant Walters, Robert Peterson, David M. Houton, and Spencer Smith, all of whom listed their address as c/o Air America, Army Post Office, San Francisco, California. Air America was the CIA airline that transported the opium out of the Golden Triangle to Saigon, Hong Kong, and Bangkok.

Also working through the Nugan Hand Bank was Edwin F. Wilson, a CIA agent involved in smuggling arms to the Middle East and later sentenced to prison by a U.S. court for smuggling illegal arms to Libya. Edwin Wilson's associate in Middle East arms shipments was Theodore Shackley, head of the CIA station in Miami, Florida. It was Shackley who, along with Rafael "Chi" Quintero, a Cuban-American, forged the plot to assassinate Fidel Castro by using organized crime figures Santo Trafficante, Jr., John Roselli, and Sam Giancana. In 1973, when William Colby became the Director of CIA, Shackley replaced him as head of covert operations for the Far East.

In 1980, the Nugan Hand Bank became unraveled. The Australian member of the Nugan Hand team, Frank Nugan, was found shot dead in his Mercedes on a remote road. In his trousers pocket was the business card of Nugan Hand Bank's lawyer, former CIA director William Colby. On the back of the card was Colby's itinerary for his upcoming trip to Australia. Next to the body was a Bible with a meat-pie wrapper marking a page. On the wrapper were the names of William Colby and Robert Wilson, a California Congressman who was then the ranking Republican member of the House Armed Services Committee.

Auditors called in to investigate the bank opened a veritable Pandora's box of crime and intrigue. Millions of dollars were missing. Many of the principal depositors of the bank were known to be connected with the international narcotics traffic in Asia and the Middle East. The CIA was using Nugan Hand Bank to finance arms smuggling and a vast array of other clandestine operations including illegal expenditures of millions of dollars on a disinformation campaign designed to unseat the liberal Australian Prime Minister, Gough Whitlam. This campaign falsely accused Whitlam of various immoral and illegal activities. Whitlam was forced to resign as Prime Minister and was replaced by a conservative Prime Minister more to the liking of the CIA. The CIA also used the Nugan Hand Bank to funnel millions of dollars into the political campaigns of politicians in other countries who supported the CIA's political views. When the true nature of the Nugan Hand Bank was made public, a CIA agent from Washington, D.C., flew to Sydney with a false passport for Michael Hand. He and Hand flew to the United States and there Michael Hand disappeared. Subsequent inquiries made of Michael Hand's father were answered with denials of any information about his son.

In short, evidence uncovered by a Government Commission in New South Wales, Australia, linked high-level CIA officials to a bank in Sydney that was responsible for financing and laundering money for a significant part of the narcotics trafficking originating in Southeast Asia (Commonwealth of New South Wales, 1982; New South Wales, 1982, 1983; Owen, 1983). It also linked the CIA to arms smuggling and illegal involvement in the democratic processes of a friendly nation. Other investigations reveal that the events in Australia were but a part of a worldwide involvement in narcotics and arms smuggling by the CIA and French intelligence (Hougan, 1978; Owen, 1983, Kruger, 1979).

Arms Smuggling

By far the most important form of state crime today is arms smuggling (NARMIC, 1984). To a significant extent, U.S. involvement in narcotics after the Vietnam War must be understood as a means of funding the purchase of military weapons for nations and insurgent groups that cannot be funded legally through congressional allocations or when U.S. law prohibits support.

In violation of U.S. law, members of the National Security Council, the Department of Defense, and the Central Intelligence Agency carried out a plan to sell millions of dollars worth of arms to Iran and use profits from the sales for illegal support of the Contras in Nicaragua (Senate Hearings, 1986). The Boland Amendment, which became effective in 1985, prohibited any direct or indirect assistance to the Contras. Cut off from any legal avenues of support, former Director of the CIA, William Casey, contacted Lieutenant Colonel Oliver North of the National Security Council. Casey instructed North to set up a self-sustaining enterprise that would be accountable to only a few people. The enterprise was allegedly led by Theodore Shackley, and its members included General Richard Secord, General John Singlaub, Thomas Clines, and other veterans of the 1961 invasion of Cuba (*The Guardian*, 1986).

United States Senator Daniel Inouye claims that this "secret government within our government" waging war in Third World countries was part of former U.S. President Ronald Reagan's foreign policy (*The Guardian*, 1987b). However, weapons were sold to Iran contrary to the Reagan Administration's official policy and the Illegal Arms Export Control Act, which made the sale of unlicensed arms to Iran unlawful and prohibited the licensing of such weapons. The weapons were obtained by the CIA through the Pentagon. U.S. Secretary of Defense, Caspar Weinberger, ordered the transfer of weapons from the Army stocks to the CIA without the knowledge of Congress on four occasions in 1986 (*The Washington Post*, 1986b). The arms were then transferred to such middlemen as Iranian arms dealers Yaacov Nimrodi and Manucher Ghorbanifar, and Saudi Arabian businessman Adnan Khashoggi. Weapons were also flown directly to the Contras and funds from their sale were diverted to provide financial support for Contra warfare (*The Washington Post*, 1986b).

The United States, through the CIA and the Drug Enforcement Administration, co-operated with narcotics smugglers in order to provide economic and military aid to the Contras in Nicaragua thus supporting their effort to overthrow the Sandinista government. In 1986, the Reagan Administration admitted that Adolfo Chamorro's Contra group, which was supported by the CIA, was helping a

Columbian drug trafficker transport drugs into the U.S. Chamorro was arrested in April 1986 for his involvement (Potter and Bullington, 1987:54; Lernoux, 1984).

At the same time that the U.S. government was supporting the Nicaraguan rebels, the administration was also launching a slanderous campaign against the Sandinistas for their supposed involvement in drug trafficking. Twice during his weekly radio broadcasts in 1986, Reagan accused the Sandinistas of smuggling drugs (*The Guardian*, 1986). In 1984, Barry Seal, an informant and pilot for the Drug Enforcement Administration, was ordered by members of the CIA and the DEA to photograph the Sandinistas loading a plane (Lee, 1987). During a televised speech in March 1986, Reagan showed this picture taken of Sandinista officials allegedly involved in drug trafficking. After the photograph was displayed, Congress passed a bill for US$100 million in aid for the Contras. Because Seal was well aware of the drug-smuggling activities of the Contra network and a Colombian cocaine magnate, he was murdered. Shortly after Seal's murder, the DEA issued a "low-key clarification" regarding the validity of the infamous photograph, but the story received little attention since Seal was already dead and the campaign for congressional money had been successful (*The Guardian*, 1987a).

John Stockwell, a former high-ranking CIA official, claims that drug smuggling and the CIA were essential components in the private campaign in support of the Contras (*The Guardian*, 1986). George Morales, one of the largest drug traffickers in South America, testified that he had been approached by the CIA in 1984 to fly weapons into Nicaragua. Morales claims that the CIA opened up an airstrip in Costa Rica and provided his pilot with information on how to avoid radar traps. According to Morales, he flew 20 weapons shipments into Costa Rica in 1984 and 1985. In return, the CIA helped him to smuggle thousands of kilograms of cocaine into the United States (Spin, 1987). Morales alone channeled US$250 000 quarterly to Contra leader, Fernando Chamorro, from his trafficking activity (Spin, 1987). Morales' pilot, Gary Betzner, has stated that he flew 4000 pounds of arms into Costa Rica and flew 500 kg of cocaine to Lakeland, Florida, on his return trips (Spin, 1987). From 1985 to 1987, the CIA arranged from 50 to 100 flights using U.S. airports where customs inspections could be avoided (Potter and Bullington, 1987:53).

The destination of Morales and Betzner's flights was the hidden airstrip on the ranch of John Hull, an admitted CIA agent who was a primary player in Oliver North's plan to aid the Contras (Spin, 1987). Hull's activities were closely monitored by Robert Owen, himself an important figure in the Contra re-support effort. Owen was in constant contact with Oliver North regarding Hull's activities and other Contra dealings (Potter and Bullington, 1987:15). Hull established the Institute for Democracy, Education, and Assistance, which has raised support for the Contras. In October 1985, Congress granted Hull's Institute US$50 000 in humanitarian aid for the Contras.

John Hull has been described as the commander of the Costa Rican branch of the Nicaraguan Democratic Forces (the FDN branch of the Contras). Not only was Hull's ranch a training base for the Contras, it was also a location from which cocaine was exported to the U.S. Hull received monthly installments of US$10 000 from the National Security Council for his participation in arms and drug smuggling (Spin, 1987).

Since 1983, North's network of operatives and mercenaries has been linked to the largest drug cartel in South America. Colombian Jorge Ochoa Vasquez, the leader of the Medellin drug empire, is responsible for supplying from 70% to 80% of the cocaine entering the United States each year. Vasquez was taken into custody by Spanish police in October 1984 when a verbal order was issued by the U.S. Embassy in Madrid for his arrest. The embassy specified that officer Cos-Gayon, who had undergone training with the Drug Enforcement Administration, perform the arrest. Other members of the Madrid Judicial Police were linked to the DEA and North's arms-smuggling network. Vasquez's lawyers informed him that the U.S. would alter his extradition if he agreed to implicate the Sandinista government in drug trafficking. Vasquez refused and spent 20 months in jail before returning to Colombia. The Spanish courts ruled that the U.S. was attempting to use Vasquez to discredit Nicaragua and accordingly he was released (Lee, 1987).

There are other links between the U.S. government and the Medellin cartel. Jose Blandon, Panamanian General Manuel Noriega's former chief adviser, claims that DEA operations protected the drug empire in the past and that the agency paid Noriega US$4.7 million for his silence. Blandon also testified in U.S. Senate committee hearings that Panama's bases were used as training camps for the Contras in exchange for "economic" support from the U.S. Furthermore, Blandon contends that the CIA gave Panamanian leaders intelligence documents involving U.S. senators and their aides. The CIA denies these charges (*The Christian Science Monitor*, 1988).

In January 1983, two Contra leaders in Costa Rica persuaded the U.S. Department of Justice to return over US$36 000 in drug profits to dealer Julio Zavala and Carlos Cabazas for aid to the Contras (Potter and Bullington, 1987).

Michael Palmer, a drug trafficker in Miami, testified that the U.S. State Department's Nicaraguan Humanitarian Assistance Office contracted with his company, Vortex Sales and Leasing, to ship aid to the Contras. Palmer claims that he smuggled US$40 million in marijuana to America between 1977 and 1985 (*The Guardian*, 1988).

There is evidence that the Drug Enforcement Administration was involved in the Iran/Contra dealings. In 1985, DEA operatives were planning to pay US$2 million in bribes and ransom to Lebanese extremists for the release of U.S. hostages. The bribe funds were obtained from Texas industrialist, Ross Perot (*The Washington Post*, 1987b).

Several Swiss bank accounts have been implicated in the transfer of arms to Iran and aid to the Contras. An article in *The Washington Post* (1986a) states that up to US$30 million was involved in the arms-for-aid transfer. Oliver North and Richard Secord established the Lake Resources account and Secord testified that US$3.5 million was diverted from this account to the Contras (*The Washington Post*, 1987a). Lake Resources was a company registered in Panama in May 1985 and frequently received deposits from Iranian and Saudi businessmen. The corporation has been linked to the CIA airstrip in Costa Rica and John Hull (*The Washington Post*, 1986b).

Three of the people involved in the illegal supply of arms to the Contras and the trade-off of drugs for guns were involved earlier in the illegal narcotics smuggling in Vietnam and or were principals in the development of the Nugan Hand Bank in Australia:

- Theodore Shackley who was with the CIA in Laos and assisted in the organization of opium trafficking, and later second in command of the CIA's clandestine operations (*Business Week*, 1986).
- Thomas Clines, a former CIA officer who worked with the Nugan Hand Bank to facilitate the takeover of a London-based bank, one of the key negotiators in the sale of arms to Iran and the Contras.

- General Richard Secord who arranged the secret bank accounts in Switzerland for transferring money from the sale of arms to the Contras. (Secord was formerly in charge of the Long Cheng base In Laos and was peripherally connected to the Nugan Hand Bank in Sydney.)

Why?

Why would U.S. government officials from the National Security Council, the Department of Defense, the Department of State, and the CIA become involved in arms and narcotics smuggling, money laundering, assassination, and other criminal activities? The answer lies in the structural contradictions that inhere in nation-states (Chambliss, 1980; Chambliss, 1987; Block and Chambliss, 1982).

As Weber, Marx, and Gramsci pointed out, no state can survive without establishing legitimacy. The law is a fundamental cornerstone in creating legitimacy and the illusion of social order. It proclaims universal principles that demand some behaviors and prohibit others. The protection of property and personal security are obligations assumed by states everywhere both as a means of legitimizing the states' franchise on violence and as a means of protecting commercial interests (Chambliss and Seidman, 1982).

The threat posed by smuggling both to personal security and to property interests makes laws prohibiting smuggling essential. Under some circumstances, however, these laws contradict other interests of the state. This contradiction prepares the ground for state-organized crime as a solution to the conflicts and dilemmas posed by the simultaneous existence of contradictory "legitimate" goals.

Since the end of World War II, the single most important concern of U.S. foreign policy has been the containment of communism. The military-intelligence establishment of the United State was given the responsibility for carrying out this policy. It has been resolutely committed to fighting the spread of "communism" throughout the world (Turner, 1985). From the point of view of those committed to this goal, the sad reality is that the Congress and the Presidency are not consistent in their provision of the money and policies thought by the front-line warriors to be necessary for the accomplishment of their lofty goals. As a result, programs are sometimes undermined by a lack of funding and even by laws that prohibit their continuation (such as Congress' passage of laws prohibiting support for the

Contras). Officials of government agencies adversely affected by political changes are thus faced with a dilemma: if they comply with the new limitations on their activities, they sacrifice their mission. The dilemma is heightened by the fact that they can anticipate future policy changes that would reinstate their resources and their freedom. When that time comes, however, programs adversely affected will be difficult if not impossible to reinstate.

Discussion

Former Assistant Attorney General of the United States, William Bradford Reynolds, inadvertently revealed the root cause of the drug problem in the U.S. in a Department of Justice memo:

> Overall, we should send the message that there are two ways to approach drugs: the soft, easy way that emphasizes drug treatment and rehabilitation versus the hard, tough approach that emphasizes strong law enforcement measures and drug testing. Naturally, we favor the latter (Reynolds, 1989).

For 70 years, law enforcement agencies in the United States have successfully lobbied for the criminalization of drugs and ever-harsher penalties for users and sellers (Musto, 1984). The fact that this policy has been a complete and utter failure should give Mr. Reynolds and all of us reason to reconsider our current approach.

Trying to solve the problems associated with the use of drugs through law enforcement agencies has led to an international crisis in governance without significantly affecting the flow of drugs or the number of people addicted (Kaplan, 1983). Instead, there has been a steady and constant increase in the availability of drugs and the number of drug users. Cocaine, crack, heroin, marijuana, hashish, legally produced (but illegally sold) amphetamines and barbiturates, and a host of "designer drugs" are as commonplace as television sets and boom-boxes in America's homes and on our streets. Drugs on university campuses and Wall Street are as readily available (and as popular) as *Playboy* magazine.

Hand-in-hand with increased use and availability has come wholesale corruption. Organized crime syndicates have grown wealthy and powerful on the profits from drug smuggling. Political candidates all over the world are bought and sold. And the most powerful intelligence agencies of the most powerful military nation in the history of the world is implicated in international narcotics trafficking in the name of "defending democracy."

Meanwhile, ever-increasing human suffering goes virtually unnoticed amidst the moral rhetoric of politicians and law enforcement spokesmen echoing the moral indignation of the alcohol prohibitionists of an earlier era.

Drugs are sold indiscriminately and with no concern for what the additives that are used to increase profits are doing to consumers. To protect their profits, crime networks employ murder, threats, blackmail, and the destruction of whole nations.

The use of illegal drugs has spread from small enclaves of addicts to every corner of society, but it is the people in the poorest sectors of society who are victimized the most (O'Mally et al., 1985). They spend their scarce resources on drugs they can ill-afford, although they are in the greatest need of the escape drugs provide by giving momentary relief from the boredom and frustration of their lives. Further, diseases such as AIDS and hepatitis are inflicted on the poor more than others as they share needles and seek bargains in inferior products.

For the taxpayer there is the awesome cost of supporting a massive and endlessly greedy law enforcement machinery that keeps promising results but delivers only more misery along with demands for ever-increasing expenditures. The existence of such a powerful, well-armed and politically persuasive police force in a democratic society is a development that should be seriously weighed and not accepted as necessary in the aftermath of anti-drug hysteria. If we know nothing else about bureaucracies we know they will never disappear or curtail their influence voluntarily. Do we want a nation bordering on a police state? Even if this were the only way to stop the drug traffic — which it is not — one wonders if it would be worth it.

Carefully ignored in all the law enforcement propaganda is the experience of the 11 states that have decriminalized marijuana. While the evidence is spotty it does suggests that the use of marijuana actually declines after legalization (see Chapter 9). Where marijuana is legal the incentive to create new markets is reduced and much of the excitement that comes from violating rules disappears.

It should be obvious to anyone who objectively reviews the history of alcohol and drug prohibition that some form of legalization is the only way to deal rationally with the drug problem. Legalizing drugs will not make them disappear any more than did the legalization of alcohol. It will, however, give us the possibility to control their abuse and to cut back on the corruption of political leaders and law enforcement agencies, to stop the devastation of entire communities, and to restore the lives of untold numbers of human beings.

Legalization should not be confused with an open invitation to consume any and all drugs indiscriminately. The highly addictive qualities of heroin make it a dangerous substance for the open marketplace. Allowing medical doctors to administer sustaining amounts to addicts, however, would greatly curtail the profits and go a long way to solve many attendant problems. Cocaine is less addictive than heroin, but for persons addicted it should be made available from medical doctors as well.

No doubt one of the deterrents to over-consumption of these drugs, as is the case with alcohol and cigarettes, is their high cost. Even though these drugs can be produced cheaply, a state-controlled system of marketing should retain a fairly high price and use the ensuing profits to set up rehabilitation and education programs. Marijuana should simply be legalized. Perhaps the California model permitting people to be in possession of less than an ounce and to grow marijuana for their own consumption would suffice to limit usage. If the profit for criminal networks were taken out of heroin, cocaine, and marijuana, much of the attendant problems described above would disappear.

It must be remembered in considering alternative social policies that an ideal solution does not exist. We must always weigh the costs and the benefits. No one can doubt that the cost of our present drug policy is excessive. Common sense, scientific knowledge, and logic all suggest that legalization is long overdue.

References

Block, Alan A. and William J. Chambliss. 1982. *Organizing Crime*. New York: Elsevier.

Business Week. 1986. "Washington Outlook: Spy vs. Spy at the CIA and NSC." December 29:45.

Chambliss, William J. 1977. "Markets, Profits, Labor and Smack." *Contemporary Crises* 1:53-57.

———. 1980. "On Law Making." *British Journal of Law and Society* 6:149-172.

Chambliss, William J., and Robert B. Seidman. 1982. *Law, Order and Power* Rev. ed. Reading, MA: Addison-Wesley.

Christian Science Monitor. 1988. "Hearings Tie Noriega To Contras and Drugs: Panamanian Bases Used for Contra Training." February 11:3 4.

Commonwealth of New South Wales. 1982. *New South Wales Joint Task Force on Drug Trafficking.* Sydney: Government of New South Wales.

Graham, James M. 1972. "Amphetamine Politics on Capitol Hill." *Transaction,* 9 (January): 14-23, 53.

The Guardian. 1986. December 31, 15.

———. 1987a. January 28, 3.

———. 1987b. July 29, 2-4.

———. 1988. March 20, 3.

Hougan, Jim. 1978. *Spooks: The Haunting of America — The Private Use of Secret Agents.* New York: William Morrow.

Kaplan, John. 1983. *The Hardest Drug: Heroin and Public Policy.* Chicago, IL: University of Chicago Press.

Kruger, Henrik. 1980. *The Great Heroin Coup.* Boston, MA: South End Press.

Lee, Martin A. 1987. "How the Drug Czar Got Away." *The Nation,* September 5:189-192.

Lernoux, Penny. 1984. "The Miami Connection." *The Nation,* February 18:186-198.

Lindesmith, Alfred R. 1969. *Opiates and the Law.* Bloomington, IN: Indiana University Press.

Maurer, Marc. 1990. *Young Black Men and the Criminal Justice System: A Growing National Problem.* Washington, D.C.: The Sentencing Project, February.

McCoy, Alfred W. 1972. *The Politics of Heroin in Southeast Asia.* New York: Harper and Row.

Musto, David. 1984. *The American Disease.* New Haven, CT: Yale University Press.

Nadelmann, Ethan. 1988. "U.S. Drug Policy: A Bad Export." *Foreign Policy* (Spring), 83-109.

NARMIC. 1984. *Military Exports to South Africa: A Research Report on the Arms Embargo.* Philadelphia, PA: American Friends Service Committee.

New South Wales. 1982. *Preliminary Report of the Royal Commission to Investigate the Nugan Hand Bank Failure.* Sydney: Federal Parliament Report, New South Wales.

———. 1983. *Royal Commission on Drug Trafficking* (interim reports). Sydney: Federal Parliament Report, New South Wales.

Nihill, Grant. 1982. "Bank Links to Spies, Drugs." *The Advertiser,* November 10.

O'Malley, Patrick M., Lloyd D. Johnston and Jerald G. Bachman. 1985. "Cocaine Use Among American Adolescents and Young Adults" in Nicholas J. Kozel and Edgar H. Adams (eds.), *Cocaine Use in America: Epidemiological and Clinical Perspectives.* National Institute of Drug Abuse Research Monograph 61. Washington, D.C.: Government Printing Office.

Owen, John. 1983. *Sleight of Hand: The $25 Million Nugan Hand Bank Scandal.* Sydney: Calporteur Press.

Potter, Gary W., and Bruce Bullington. 1987. "Drug Trafficking and the Contras: A Case of State Organized Crime." Paper presented at annual meeting of the American Society of Criminology, Montreal.

Reynolds, William Bradford. 1989. *Confidential Memo.* Washington, D.C.: U.S. Attorney General's Office.

Senate Hearings. 1986. *Senate Select Committee on Assassination, Alleged Assassination Plots Involving Foreign Leaders. Interim Report of the Senate Select Committee to Study Governmental Operations With Respect to Intelligence Activities.* 94th Cong., 1st sess., November 20, Washington, D.C.: Government Printing Office.

Spin. 1987. "Cuban Liberation and Drug Trafficking in Miami." May: 59-67.

Turner, Stansfield. 1985. *Secrecy and Democracy: The CIA in Transition.* New York: Houghton Mifflin.

Washington Post. 1986a. "Up to $30 Million Transferred: Deposits Made During Congress Ban on Aid to Rebels." November 26: A Section, 1.

———. 1986b. "Yaacov Nimrodi: A Tale of Arms and the Man." December 14: Outlook Section, 1.

———. 1987a. "Sultan's Gift Went to Wrong Account; Brunei Leader Contributed $10 Million as 'Bridge' for Contras." May 13: A Section, 1.

———. 1987b. The Iran-Contra hearings, May 14: A Section, 16.

2

Drugs and Social Control in Scandinavia: A Case Study in International Moral Entrepreneurship

Jørgen Jepsen

Seen from an international perspective, the Scandinavian countries as a group seem homogeneous with respect to drug control policy. The absence of capital punishment and the infrequent resort to long prison sentences make Scandinavia appear to "lag behind" a good deal of the rest of the world. Moreover, when compared to the level of drug use and crime in such places as the U.S. and Latin America, Scandinavia represents a relatively peaceful picture.

On closer examination, however, Scandinavia increasingly seems to be imitating the patterns of the outside world. For instance, the differences between Denmark, on the one hand, and Norway and Sweden, on the other — differences that are rather remarkable in alcohol control systems, for example — are increasingly narrowing as a result of pressures both from within Scandinavia itself and from outside. This movement towards convergence of drug control policy is due in large part to (1) a general trend in the direction of closer international co-operation, evidenced by a new United Nations convention on illegal drugs, and (2) an increase in the moralistic tenor of public discourse on drugs in Scandinavia and the rest of the world. Legal changes such as Sweden's criminalization of drug use in 1988, and crusading slogans such as the call for a "drug-free Scandinavia by 1990" are local examples of this development.

As a result of such pressures, indigenous ways of dealing with drug problems in Scandinavia are being overwhelmed by the repressive weight of international condemnatory and control-oriented approaches. A preference for repression through legislation, law enforcement, and imprisonment increasingly militates against "softer" approaches, including those based on community self-help and alternative treatment measures.

Drug Control Policy Differences Within Scandinavia

The Scandinavian nations exhibit striking differences in their traditions of official reaction to social deviance. These differences are clearly manifest in the region's drug control policies, most notably in the field of alcohol control. Finland, Norway, and Sweden have strict alcohol control systems based on state (licensed) monopolies for the production and/or distribution of alcohol, on detailed regulations governing the consumption of alcohol in restaurants, and on controls over the retail distribution of beer. Denmark, on the other hand, allows nearly free production, importation, and distribution of alcohol. The main policy instruments in Denmark for limiting alcohol use are a combination of education (factual information on alcohol and its effects) and a relatively high alcohol tax. Immediately after its introduction in 1917, taxation led to such a considerable drop in alcohol consumption that ever since it has been almost the only preventive measure.

In approaching the control of alcoholism, Denmark for many years has based intervention on voluntary measures, whereas Norway and Sweden have strong traditions of compulsory treatment, including Norway's *Opstad* (repealed, however, in 1970 after considerable public pressure) and numerous Swedish laws that call for compulsory treatment. The different national traditions regarding social control have led Scandinavians to engage in scornful mutual reproach and criticism. Thus, Denmark is seen as "intolerably permissive" by many Finns, Swedes, and Norwegians, whereas Danes speak contemptu-ously of "Control Sweden" and view Norwegian alcohol laws mainly as a reflection of an antiquated social conservatism.

In terms of alcohol consumption in Scandinavian countries, Denmark is clearly the country with the highest level, but this is viewed by Danes as a reflection of their society's more cosmopolitan ways owing to geographical location and a relatively high level of social mobility. As for Denmark's alleged level of alcohol "abuse," Danes are skeptical of the other Nordic countries' contention that there is a direct and constant relationship between alcohol abuse and the level of consumption. The problems of alcohol abusers are seen by Danes as more or less independent of the dominant continental alcohol culture within their country.

The differences in national traditions may be noted also in the Danes' more liberal attitudes toward other forms of social deviance. The "flower-power" generation of the 1960s and 1970s was much more prominent in Denmark than in the other Nordic countries. Public disorder in the streets and elsewhere continues to be more common in Denmark, and Danish public discourse on drug control policy is characterized by both liberal and conservative arguments, but with a long tradition for the reduction of punitiveness. A pragmatic or problem-solving view of criminal justice policy characterizes Denmark, in opposition to the moralistic tradition of Norway, the technical-intellectual "social engineering" tradition of Sweden, and the strong Finnish predilection for penal institutions.

In terms of crime (as officially measured), Sweden takes the lead, followed rather closely by Denmark, with Finland and Norway well behind. In addition, as indicated previously, social deviance is not viewed as so much of a problem in Denmark as in the more traditional Nordic societies. Moreover, for the last 100 years Danish policies have been free of influence by religious and temperance groups or party politicians, as is characteristic of, in particular, Swedish and Norwegian political life. Although Denmark has had a Christian People's Party for at least 20 years, its influence has been limited. In recent years, however, the party has begun to manifest itself more forcefully in two areas of great public concern: (1) the environment (for several years the Christian People's Party has occupied the cabinet post of Minister for the Environment), and (2) alcohol and drug control policy.

In the late 1960s, when new life-styles were introduced into the country, Denmark's well-deserved reputation for tolerance of social diversity also characterized its reaction to drug use. The use of cannabis was handled rather leniently by the criminal justice system, with police measures and court sentences relatively mild until about 1968. In any case, problems associated with drug use were less prominent in those years. For several years, Denmark retained the Euphoriant Drugs Act of 1955 with its upper limit of two years' imprisonment.

But as the youth movement, and in particular the "hippie" subculture, grew and became more visible, illegal drug use was increasingly seen as a social problem. The nontraditional "alternative institutions", such as the Copenhagen Youth Clinic, fought a losing battle in the drug debate against the "hawks" led by a Copenhagen chief prosecutor and other moral entrepreneurs, including some very active and verbal parental groups.

In 1969, under heavy pressure from the other Scandinavian countries, Denmark added a special section (Section 191) to the Danish Criminal Code providing a maximum penalty of six years for "professional drug trafficking." In 1975, this was amended with a subsection (Section 191, Subject 1, Paragraph 2) that addressed cases with "aggravating circumstances," that is, cases involving "a considerable quantity of a particularly dangerous or harmful drug". In these cases the maximum penalty was increased to ten years' imprisonment. Furthermore, in cases of "particularly aggravating circumstances," that is, where several instances of trafficking have come up for adjudication at the same time, the maximum penalty could be raised to "exceed the most severe penalty prescribed for any of the offenses by up to a half" (Section 88, Danish Criminal Code). At the time, these changes were in keeping with those elsewhere in Scandinavia, but since then Norway, without consulting Denmark, has changed (in 1981 and 1984) its penal code to allow for a maximum penalty of 21 years' imprisonment for the most serious cases.

Sentencing practices in Danish courts reveal a steady rise in prison sentences for drug trafficking, consistent with the "war on drugs" inspired by the U.S. and the campaigns for "a drug-free society" in Sweden and Norway. This may result in new demands to raise the penalty limits to those of Norway, since the upper limit of the penalty framework in Denmark has now been stretched several times (see Kruse, 1987).

Denmark has no criminal penalties for the sale of hypodermic needles and other paraphernalia used in the consumption of drugs, although such goods may be seized and confiscated in drug cases.

Nor is there any penalty for "fostering the use of drugs." Advertising is prohibited only if it involves drugs that are fraudulently alleged to have beneficial health effects (fraudulent advertising of medical substances). In actual practice, hypodermic needles are presently available from vending machines in Copenhagen, Aarhus, and Odense as a means to combat the spread of AIDS. In recent months, 16 000 needles per month were being handed out free of charge in Copenhagen alone.[1] However, the use of hypodermic needles is still illegal in prison where they are seized and confiscated as contraband. A drive for supplying free hypodermic needles to prisoners, promoted by the official National Board on Alcohol and Drugs, has been turned down on several occasions by prison authorities on the ground that, since drug use in prison is illegal, it would be inappropriate to dispense drug paraphernalia to inmates.

In 1988, after a heated parliamentary debate in which views akin to those characterizing the American "war on drugs" movement ultimately proved decisive, Sweden made drug use punishable, thus joining Norway, Finland, and Greece in criminalizing illegal drug use. The official Danish position, however, is that drug use *in and of itself* should not be punished. The sole exception to this principle is in regard to "possession" of drugs. Penalties for possession depend on the amount seized and circumstances surrounding the arrest, that is, whether possession is deemed to be for personal use or for trafficking. The latter is assumed if the seizure involves a large quantity. Historically, the ban on possession has been seen as a way to circumvent the burden of proof relating to trafficking when otherwise not proved. Still, possession of even 0.5 mg of heroin and 0.5 g of cannabis, amounts not reasonably associated with trafficking, is regularly punishable.

Denmark's liberal tradition has resulted in a distinction between cannabis and "hard" drugs in both the criminal code and in the practices of police and prosecutors. In practice, minor cannabis offenses are normally dealt with by means of small fines or suspended sentences. The distinction was first evidenced in a circular issued in 1969 by the Danish Attorney General as a precondition for a parliamentary compromise to stiffen penalties in respect of other drugs.[2] This circular has been the object of repeated attacks by Denmark's drug policy "hawks" since that time, by other Scandinavian countries and, among others, by the Christian People's Party in Denmark.

Section 191 of the Danish Criminal Code makes a distinction between "particularly dangerous or harmful drugs" and other illegal drugs. Similarly, the Euphoriant Drugs Act distinguishes between those drugs that are "exceptionally dangerous" and those that are "dangerous." Technically speaking, cannabis is still regarded as a "dangerous" drug since it has no legal use. In actual practice, however, cannabis is regarded as a rather less than "dangerous" drug. This practical understanding was further strengthened in the circular issued in 1969 by the Attorney General which established some fundamental policy guidelines for the police and prosecutors when dealing with cannabis offenses.

Both Norway and Sweden have compulsory treatment programs for drug addicts. Some of these programs, in the form of psychiatric treatment, are pursuant to a special law on compulsory internment, while others are pursuant to the law on minors. Collective treatment facilities, such as those found in Hassela in Sweden and in Hov in Norway, have been cited as models for Denmark to emulate. However, to date no such institutions have been established in Denmark, but a proposal for a law on "contractual treatment" will be considered by the Danish Parliament in the spring of 1992.

It is clear that significant differences exist, both historically and currently, among the Scandinavian countries in relation to their policies on the control of intoxicants, be they alcohol or drugs. These differences were acknowledged in a Danish policy statement relating to "Target 17" of the World Health Organization's program, "Health for All 2000." While the Danish statement focused mainly on alcohol policy, it was also directed at other drugs. In April 1988, the Chairman of the Danish Council on Alcohol and Narcotics stated:

In Target 17, the World Health Organization points to the importance of efforts to reduce the use of alcohol and other noxious substances [the latter phrase is often omitted in the debate] by at least 25% up until year 2000 . . . The Council on Alcohol and Narcotics is not of the opinion that the problems are to be found exclusively in the bottle or in the syringe. The problems arise in the interaction in the dynamics . . . between people, the contents of bottles and syringes and society . . . My advice, consequently, should be that we avoid focusing too narrowly on the quantitative goal of Target 17. (Opening Address to the Annual Assembly on Alcohol and Narcotics, Copenhagen, April 1988)

The Danish Minister of Health later commented:

I fully agree. In my opinion, Target 17 must be seen in the context in which it stands, namely in the section on life-style. I, too, would rather see us concentrating on the basic conditions, thus aiming at reducing the damage related to intoxicants, and in the long run the consumption. It is a question whether Target 17 doesn't in reality confuse goals and means. (Alcohol and Drug Council: Contribution to the Preparation of the Prevention Planning of the Ministry of Health, Copenhagen, September 28, 1988, p. 8)

In November 1988 the Council on Alcohol and Narcotics summarized the political dimension of Danish alcohol policy as follows:

The means to be used are: fiscal policy measures, education, information, preventive work, and treatment. It is not considered desirable to apply more restrictions or prohibitions than broad popular support can be found for. In other words, a liberal alcohol policy implies the exclusion of several of the measures which, for example, the other Nordic countries apply. (Minutes of the Meeting of the Alcohol and Drug Council, Copenhagen, November 29, 1988).

In Denmark, it is clear that a distinction is still drawn, by both the general public and government officials, between alcohol policies and those for drugs. But Denmark's attempts to follow its own line of policy are under much greater pressure when it comes to drugs than to alcohol.

Pressures Toward Conformity

In Scandinavia there is a tradition of regional co-operation on penal policy, as well as on such fields as environmental protection, cultural co-operation, social policy, and social services. The Nordic Council is a forum for the exchange of views and policy co-ordination, based on reports by experts and parliamentary cross-national committees. Proposals in the Nordic Council may lead to parallel legislative initiatives, as well as preparatory level research projects and fact-finding efforts. One such initiative is the plan for "A drug-free Scandinavia."[3]

Such attempts at bringing national policies in line with those of neighboring countries go hand-in-hand with other international movements to establish joint standards. In the field of drug control policy, however, the Nordic debates have received a clear impetus from Swedish and Norwegian religious and temperance party members. The strong moralistic tone of Nordic proposals and policy statements have left little room for doubts about the possible effectiveness of relevant measures or possible side effects of increasing legal repression. The marked preference for strong controls in Finland, Norway, and Sweden, derived from their efforts regarding alcohol, have left little room for discussions of possible alternatives to drug control policies. More often than not, discussions have centered upon statements of principles rather than upon careful weighing of advantages and disadvantages of alternative strategies.

Thus far, standardization of criminal law in Nordic countries has gone only so far as agreement on appropriate levels of legal penalties. In spite of pressures for unity, Denmark retains a maximum penalty of ten years' imprisonment and, for the moment, offers no reason for change. Discussions center instead on relevant police measures, including the use of undercover agents, wiretaps[4] and anonymous witnesses. Denmark seems more prone than its neighbors to disregard traditional legal safeguards and reservations about due process.[5] In this regard, Denmark is more "continental" or "modern" than its Scandinavian counterparts, but even here convergence is becoming the norm.

The Narcotics Police lobby, active in all Scandinavian countries, exerts steady pressure on government to win authority for ever-increasing extraordinary legal powers and "untraditional measures of investigation." A powerful alliance comprising police, politicians and moral entrepreneurs is exerting influence on the criminal justice system, and at times on the legislative level as well.

On the other hand, political voices are seldom heard advocating less repressive measures and reconsideration of the social costs of repressive control. Even when they do speak out, they are often labeled by officials as "irresponsible," notwithstanding growing doubts among even high-level representatives of the criminal justice system regarding the efficacy of repression. Nevertheless, in Scandinavia, the concept of "control damage" is being increasingly advocated at the academic level and in scientific publications (Winsløw 1984, 1987; Nebelong, 1987; Jepsen 1989).

What Is Control Damage?

The concept of "control damage," or unintended negative side effects of repressive drug control policies, was first developed in the mid-1980s by Winsløw (1984) and Bruun and Christie (1985). Control damage was one of the main topics of a seminar organized in 1985 by the Nordic Council through the Scandinavian Research Council for Criminology (Narkotika og kontrolpolitik, 1985). One outcome of this conference was the proposal for a joint Scandinavian study of the effects of drug control policies in the Nordic countries. This study is presently being conducted.[6]

An outline indicating some of the ideas underlying the term "control damage" is presented in Table 1 in the form of a cost-benefit analysis. The purpose is to indicate that for each benefit (economic, social, or ideological), there is likely to be a corresponding cost.

Table 1 Drug Control Policy Cost-Benefit Schedule

Derived (indirect) benefits	Improved social integration. Preservation of traditional society. Better health.	Increased income for pharmacies, medical industry, doctors and the state.
Direct benefits	Development of perceptions and attitudes against drugs and (ab)users. More effective repression resulting in fewer use(rs) and fewer abuse(rs).	Limitation of production, distribution and sale of illegal drugs.
Direct costs	Increase in alternative pattern of (ab)use of legal drugs, including over prescription, alcohol abuse and glue sniffing. Also possible increases in poly-drug use and "designer" drugs.	Increase in expenditure for such things as drug education, welfare aid, police, courts, prisons and drug treatment.
Derived (indirect) costs	More physical and social misery for addicts. Over concern with the drugs and symptoms of abuse. A "control-society" with less "rule of law" (due process). Promotion of prohibition as a means of solving social problems.	Higher prices of illegal drugs, more crime. Creation of a strong basis for organized crime (gangsterism). Increased police corruption.

Clearly, it is impossible to calculate or weigh such factors in precise mathematical terms: the items do not constitute a comparable scale, making difficult any attempt to "measure" them. Nor can the economic costs and benefits be computed or compared, since many of the items are of unknown magnitude and subject to popular as well as scientific misrepresentation. Yet, despite such analytical shortcomings, the figure serves as an approximation to the functional trade-offs involved.

Although some success has been achieved in halting the deterioration of due process in Denmark, particularly in drug cases, police and prosecutors still exert considerable advocacy for the expansion of "untraditional investigation measures." The safeguarding of due process in Denmark and other countries adopting these measures is put seriously at risk by the use of taps on telephones, unreasonably long periods of pre-trial detention in order to obtain confessions, the increased resort to *agents provocateurs* and the use of indictments with unacceptably low evidentiary standards. An exacerbating result of such lowering of standards is that it may become acceptable practice in other types of criminal cases. The list may not seem impressive to those living in countries that have already adopted repressive drug control policies, but to Scandinavians it represents a rather drastic change in the traditional way of perceiving due process.

On an ideological level, the most serious problem may be the damage arising from the belief that legal proscriptions can effectively contain social conflicts. Stubborn disregard for the growing evidence of social costs associated with repressive drug control policies increasingly supports the resort to measures that, rather than instruments for social reform, become mere expressions of moral sentiment. It is not new to suggest that legislation in many instances may be considered as symbolic acts with expressive purposes rather than rational means of attaining desired social reform. However, even the most "expressive" legislators should be willing to face reality and consider whether their legislative effort may not ultimately undermine the very values it is thought to uphold (Gunnlaugsson and Galliher, 1986).

International Co-Operation and Moral Imperialism

Intra-Scandinavian pressures leading to increasingly repressive drug control policies, and the moral entrepreneurship of numerous Swedes and Norwegians in relation to Danish policies, have parallels on the international scene as illustrated within the European Council and the United Nations convention preparations in Vienna.

Behind the drive for European, and even global, unity in confronting international drug trafficking, we find the same tendencies to combine tough-minded "crime fighting" with moral (and, at times, economic) imperialism, using the moral panic surrounding the growing use of illegal drugs as a vehicle for international co-operation between police and even military forces.

From the view of a small Scandinavian country with a liberal tradition of responding to social problems, the Single Convention and the Convention on Psychotropic Substances have meant a growing disregard for Denmark's approach toward social control. Alternative solutions, or even alternative perceptions, of "the drug problem" have been rejected out of hand in the face of the putative need for international solidarity.

The Vienna United Nations convention on drugs involves a further major step in the direction of reliance on repression as a means of control. Such an approach will inevitably carry with it prospects for increased control damage on a global level.

First, the numbers and types of substances subject to control are increased greatly and given a delimitation so wide as to be virtually meaningless. It is hardly an exaggeration to suggest that all chemicals that may be "used in the illicit processing or manufacture of narcotic drugs or psychotropic substances" (for example, acetone) now may be subject to criminalization.[7]

Second, the concept of "drug trafficking" is given such a wide scope through the expansive formulations in the draft convention that it involves almost no limitations to guard against abuse by the legal system.[8]

Third, the expansion of discretionary police powers with attendant potential for abuse of civil rights, advocated in the name of societal protection, is presumably made more acceptable to countries harboring reservations through a series of "safety-valve clauses." The assurance is that in each case the convention's provisions shall be interpreted in accordance with national legislation and judicial principles, so as not to conflict with the rule of law as perceived by the signatory countries. Strictly speaking, however, such clauses may render the entire convention meaningless. Yet, on a pragmatic level, international pressure may become so powerful that few countries will be able to resist and adhere to their own principles of law.

International Solidarity and the Research Community

The prediction that international co-operation in drug control policy may lead to a global indulgence in wishful thinking and unrealistic, yet powerful, moral imperialism, implies a special responsibility for social scientists within the field of deviance and social control. If one disagrees with the prediction or, after a careful weighing of the evidence, concludes that benefits clearly outweigh costs in this gigantic experiment with society and its legal system, one may support further development of international co-operation in the field of drug control policy.

However, if one agrees with the prediction or is ready to consider alternative ways of perceiving and solving the problems associated with drug use, it is of the utmost importance to speak out against the risks of a giant collective mistake.

As Sebastian Scherer (1979) has said in connection with German anti-terrorist legislation, we may be operating in a veritable "state of siege," in which misgivings are seen as treacherous alliance with or sympathy for the "enemy." Nevertheless, social scientists operating within the field of the sociology of law will betray their discipline if they cease to assail the "storm troopers" of repressive drug policy. In essence, any lesser strategy would be tantamount to surrender.

Notes

1.   Dr. Michael von Magnus, Danish Health Director, interview in Jyllands Posten (Daily News), Arhus, Denmark, June 14, 1988.

2.   The distinction between cannabis (the only illegal drug expressly regarded as "soft") and other drugs is explained further in the 1969 administrative ordinance of the Danish Attorney General, the main points of which are summarized by Kruse (1987) as follows:

Purchase, reception, and possession of drugs shall be dealt with by the police with a warning, provided it concerns drugs exclusively for one's own use. In the case of a second or subsequent, more serious crime and in the case of repeated possession of drugs other than cannabis, the offender shall be liable to a fine. The same applies to distribution or sale of minor quantities of cannabis, provided that the situation must be considered one of a single or a few isolated cases of distribution (for example, among school fellows or in youth cliques). Suspended sentence, if necessary in connection with a supplementary fine, may be imposed for a first time sale of cannabis, when the total payment does not exceed 1.000 kr., unless aggravating circumstances exist, as, for instance, distribution of considerable amounts to children under the age of 16. An ordinary penalty (that is, normal imprisonment) may be imposed in cases which concern the distribution of other drugs, unless the circumstances (especially the age of the offender) speak in favor of a suspended sentence, if necessary with conditions of drug treatment. In these cases the charge is to be brought according to the Act on Drug Control.

If the criminal offense concerns circulation (smuggling, buying, etc.) of heroin or of other drugs apart from cannabis to a greater number of persons or in return for a considerable payment, a charge must be brought for an offense against Section 191 of the Criminal Code. Smuggling or distribution of cannabis shall only be dealt with under this provision in the case of commercially organized smuggling etc. of cannabis to an extent exceeding 10 to 15 kg. In all the cases the drugs must be seized and confiscated.

This circular has been fundamental in the Danish penal policy in relation to drugs, as, for the purpose of prosecution and the penalty demands of the prosecutors, it draws an important distinction between cannabis and other drugs. It was promulgated in connection with the introduction of the six-year penalty in the Criminal Code in 1969 and presented to the legislature as a draft. This was the price paid by the law enforcement-oriented "hawks" in order to achieve the higher penalties introduced in the Criminal Code. Since 1969 it has been under repeated attacks from the "hawks," who want cannabis use treated more harshly, in part because of assumed inherent damaging effects, in part because of the "stepping stone" hypothesis.

3. Meeting of the Nordic Ministers, Stockholm, 1982. Recommendation 14/1982, 9/1984, and Proposal B 57/S by the Council of Ministers for a Nordic plan of action against narcotics (Reykjavik, December 12, 1984), and Report of the Social and Environmental Committee of January 31, 1985.

4. Wiretapping has undergone a considerable upswing since 1975, expressly as a means to deal with drug cases. From 30 in 1975 and around 330 in 1982, the annual number of court orders allowing wiretapping rose to around 700 in 1985. Of these a total of some 95% concern drugs (Preben Wilhjelm, Institute of Criminal Science, Copenhagen).

5. The main events and rules in this matter concern parliamentary regulations passed in 1985/86 after much heated debate. The most important practical result of the modification was that only policemen may be used as agents. In the police practices that had developed during preceding years, various types of agents and informers had been used, some of them former drug offenders on parole. Whereas the opposition

to "controlled delivery" was relatively minor, the regulations were framed in such a way as to avoid the police becoming participants in fostering drug offenses or characterizing such offenses as more serious or wider than would be the case had an agent not intervened. Furthermore, the use of agents avoided judicial review.

Against strong opposition from the right wing, the left side in Parliament 1986 also managed to pass an act that outlawed totally the use of "anonymous witnesses," that is, witnesses whose names were not to be known by the defendant, who was not even allowed insight into statements presented by witnesses. Defense counsel was allowed such knowledge, but could not discuss it with a client. Before the act was passed, this procedural innovation had been accepted by a Supreme Court decision in a much discussed case. The act prohibited this practice, although it was later slightly changed so that the list of witnesses with addresses could not be known to the defendant (only to the counsel for the defense.) Instead, now, in cases where witnesses are afraid of giving testimony, the prosecution may provide the witness with a new identity and pay for a relocation, a novelty which has been applied in drug cases as well as in those against rocker gangs (the Danish equivalent of the American Hell's Angels).

Thus, although some success has been achieved in halting the deterioration of due process, police and prosecutors still exert considerable pressure for expansion of such "untraditional investigation measures."

6.   Application of February 12, 1988.

7.   United Nations E.C.O.S.O.C. Document E./CONF. 82/83, 20. July 1988. Draft Convention re Article 8/27 (pp. 66-68), Article 2/18 (pp. 52-53).

8.   Draft Convention, Article 1/11.

References

Bruun, Kettil and Nils Christie. 1985. *Den gode Fiende* (The Ideal Enemy). Oslo: Universitetsforlaget.

Gunnlaugsson, Helgi and John F. Galliher. 1986. "Prohibition of Beer in Iceland: An International Test of Symbolic Politics." *Law & Society Review* 20: 335-353.

Jepsen, Jørgen. 1989. "Drug Policies in Denmark," paper presented at the Conference on Drug Policies in Western Europe, Tillburg, 1988. See also: Hans Jörg Albrecht and Anton van Kalmthout (eds.), "Drug Policies in Western Europe, *Criminological Research Reports*, Max Planck Institute for Foreign and International Penal Law, Freiburg im Breisgau Vol. 41, 1989, pp. 107-141.

Kruse, S. Vinding. 1987. "Drug Criminality from a Legal Point of View" in Per Strangeland (ed.), *Drugs and Drug Control in Scandinavia, Scandinavian Studies in Criminology* Vol. 8, Oslo: Norwegian University Press/Oxford University Press, pp. 34-52.

Narkotika Og Kontrolpolitik. 1985. Rapport fra et seminar i Rønne, Denmark, 1985 ("Drugs and Control Policy," report from a seminar at Rønne) Nordiska Rådet and Nordisk Samarbejdsråd for Kriminologi (Nordic Council and Scandinavian Research Council for Criminology, Stockholm).

Nebelong, Henrik. 1987. Oversaettelse af telefon- og rumaflytninger (translation of telephone and room tapping). *Ugeskrift for Retsvæsen* (Weekly Law Journal) 1987 B, p. 210.

Scherer, Sebastian. 1979. "Law Making in a State of Siege: Some Regularities in the Legislative Response to Political Violence." *Working Papers in European Criminology* No. 1, European Group for the Study of Deviance and Social Control, Vienna.

Jyllands-Posten (Daily Newspaper, Aarhus, Denmark). 1988. Interview with Dr. Michael von Magnus, Danish Health Director, June 14.

Wilhjelm, Preben. 1988. *Tvangsindgreb i strafferetsplejen 1976-85.* Jurist- og Økonomforbundets Forlag (Jurists' and Economists' Association, publishers), Copenhagen. (Arrest, Detention and Other Procedural Measures.)

Winsløw, Jacob Hilden. 1984. *Narreskibet (The Ship of Fools).* Holte: Forlaget SocPol.

———. 1987. Drug Abuse Treatment as a Cause of Excess Mortality among Danish Drug Abusers" in Per Stangeland (ed.), *Drugs and Drug Control in Scandinavia, Scandinavian Studies in Criminology* Vol. 8, Oslo:

3

Drugs and the Law in Post-Franco Spain

Axel R. Reeg

During a 1986 election campaign, a member of the Spanish Parliament claimed that the Secretary of State for International Relations was regularly using cocaine. The Secretary considered this a defamation of character, sued the M.P. for damages and asked a Madrid civil court for retraction (*El País*, 1988e). The court's judgment was somewhat surprising: the M.P. was ordered to retract his unproved allegation but the Secretary's claim for compensation was dismissed as unfounded. In the court's opinion the fact that one is said to be a user of illicit drugs does not constitute an injury to one's honor or reputation. The court held that drug use was considered a normal habit by wide sectors of society and therefore, in the Secretary's case, could not be seen to have damaged his honor (*El País*, 1988p). Although this judgment has been considered incorrect by many Spanish lawyers, the court's decision points out quite clearly that drugs have become a part of everyday life in Spain. Indeed, in recent years, Spain has acquired a reputation as Europe's most important drug center.

In order to understand how this state of affairs has come about, we must examine the economic and social conditions in Post-Franco Spain, as well as a number of historical and cultural conditions that have shaped Spanish society.

First, keep in mind that Spain has become a democratic country only in the past 17 years. When the Spanish dictator, General Franco, died in 1975, his legacy included a public attitude of absolute intolerance of any form of drug use. Nevertheless, drug use existed as a sign of protest against political repression. Once liberated from dictatorship, the Spaniards acquired a sense of freedom to do whatever they wanted to. It was an attitude, some would say, reflecting an anarchist tradition that has long been characteristic of Spain. There can be little doubt, however, that, since Franco's death, an absence of overt political repression has had a profound impact on Spanish society and public attitudes, including those towards drugs (Serrano Gómez, 1983:273-309).

A second significant change in the Post-Franco era has been Spain's rapid economic development during recent years. Spain's economic growth rate, about 5% for 1987 and 1988 (*El País*, 1988p), places it at the top in Europe (*Süeddeutsche Zeitung*, 1988a), while during the same period inflation has been reduced to around 5%, relatively low in contrast to much higher rates (nearly 15%) in the early 1980s (*El País*, 1988q). Moreover, the fact that Spanish businesses have been able to quadruple employers' benefits during the last two years suggests that Spain is fast becoming a prosperous society (*El País*, 1988x).

As impressive as these achievements are, in reality only a fraction of Spanish society has benefited from the new wealth. A great number of people are still unable to live up to their expectations of full participation in the new consumer society. Today in Spain there are nearly three million unemployed workers, about 20% of the active population (*El País*, 1988m), the highest unemployment rate in the European Economic Community (*El País*, 1988k). Among those below 25 years of age, the situation is even worse, with more than 30% of them jobless (*El País*, 1988b). In some regions, unemployment exceeds 50%. Given Spain's inadequate social welfare system (by European standards), all this leads, if not to an expansion of poverty, then to a high potential for drug use among a disillusioned generation that perceives a bleak future for itself.

Third, the historical and cultural diversity of Europe has given rise to different patterns of drug use throughout the Continent. The various European countries reveal a remarkable diversity in preferences for illegal drugs, offering in turn diverse market opportunities for suppliers. For instance, Spain's long-established cultural, political, and economic links with Latin America strongly influence its patterns of drug use and its drug market. Furthermore, a combination of poverty and political repression during the two decades after World War II led thousands of Spaniards to emigrate to Latin America in search of a better life. Thus, as a result of its strong ties with Latin America, Spain has developed as a major market for Columbian cocaine.

Finally, Spain is also part of what has been called "the porous south" (Dickey, 1990:22-23). With thousands of kilometers of uncontrolled coastline, close proximity to North Africa, and a traditionally relaxed attitude towards immigration, Spain is an easy mark for smugglers. Until 1990, for instance, neither Spain nor Italy required visas for short-term visitors from North Africa. In effect, anyone who could afford to buy a ticket could enter these two countries. As a result of these and other factors, there is little prospect that Spanish customs officers can control the flow of contraband into Spain.

Drug Use in Spain

One means for determining the nature and extent of a community's drug problem is to examine the amount and types of drugs seized by authorities. In this respect, the late 1980s witnessed huge increases in drug seizures by Spanish officials. In September 1987, the Spanish police proudly announced the seizure of 50 kg of cocaine. At that time it represented the "biggest [seizure] ever made" (*El País*, 1987a). In April 1988 this record was exceeded tenfold when 562 kg of cocaine were seized (*El País*, 1988a). Just a few weeks later one *ton* of pure cocaine was seized by officials (*El País*, 1988d). This was followed by the seizure of 17 tons of cannabis in July (*El País*, 1988h).

Another indirect measure of increasing drug use in Spain is the number of arrests for drug trafficking. The arrest rate for suspected drug traffickers in 1985 was 12.9 per 100 000. By 1987, the arrest rate had increased to 25.5 per 100 000, nearly double in just two years. The Spanish government estimated the number of regular drug users in Spain to be quite high by European standards. A study conducted in 1985 by the Ministry of Health estimated 1.2 to 1.8 million cannabis users (around 4% of the population), 80 000 to 125 000 heroin users, and 60 000 to 80 000 cocaine users (Ministerio de Sanidad y Consumo, 1985). In particular, the use of cocaine has increased dramatically since 1985 (*El País Domingo*, 1988a). Compared to an estimated two million Spanish alcoholics (more than 5% of the population), these figures, except as regards cannabis, might seem negligible. In the European context, however, they are among the highest rates.

Notwithstanding these findings, the effect of illicit drugs on Spain's overall mortality rate is negligible. In 1988 approximately 250 persons died from heroin use (*El País*, 1988u). While this is not an insignificant number, it should be noted that nearly 40 000 Spaniards die each year as a result of smoking tobacco (*El País Domingo*, 1988b).

The really alarming effects of illegal drug use in Spain are to be found in other areas. As elsewhere in the world, addicts need large amounts of money to pay for their drugs and, as a result, frequently turn to crime to support their habits (*El País*, 1989a). Purse snatchings, assaults and armed robberies have become increasingly common occurrences in many Spanish cities. In 1987, violent crime accounted for a shocking 70% of the total reported crime (*El País*, 1988o). Approximately two-thirds of all offenses have been attributed to drug addicts (*El País*, 1988u).

In the past decade, increasing numbers of poorly paid police (*El País*, 1988f), customs (*El País*, 1988c) and prison officers (*El País*, 1988j) have discovered that drug trafficking is an easy and relatively safe way to improve their incomes. In some instances, this phenomenon has led to a blurred distinction between "law enforcement official" and "organized criminal" (*El País*, 1988z; *El País*, 1988l).

The Spanish have come to call this relatively new situation *inseguridad ciudadana* (public insecurity), and it has brought with it public demands for stern action. In the first place, there is a growing call for harsher penalties for convicted drug users (*El País*, 1987b). Growing public insecurity has also contributed to a boom in the number of private security firms established to serve businesses and individuals alike. Additional unforeseen problems have arisen since these security companies and their employees are not under the authority of state police laws and therefore cannot be easily controlled (*El País*, 1988g).

Finally, as increasing numbers of drug offenders are incarcerated there is likely to be a growing drug problem within Spain's jails and prisons. Currently, between 60% (de la Cuesta Arzamendi, 1988) and 80% (Beristain Ipiña, 1985) of Spanish prison inmates are thought to be heroin addicts, requiring continued access to the drug by whatever means available.

Illegal Drugs and the Spanish Penal Code

Spanish drug control policy during the last decade has been marked by two important reforms, namely, the penal code provisions regarding drug offenses in 1983 (*Ley Orgánica*, 1983) and again in 1988 (*Ley Orgánica*, 1988). Before the 1983 reform, Spanish drug law was comparatively weak. The old law (Article 344 of the 1944 Penal Code) left unusually wide discretion to judges in the determination of prison sentences which could range from six months to 20 years (Reeg, 1987:662). Article 344 of the 1944 Penal Code also failed to differentiate among punishable offenses, which included producing, transporting, possessing, selling, and trafficking of illicit drugs.

In 1982, the Spanish Socialist Party gained a comfortable majority in Parliament and made a number of improvements in Spain's laws. Among these was the reform of the Criminal Drug Law in 1983. At the time of its passage the new drug law was one of the most progressive in Europe.

The 1983 Criminal Drug Law contained a number of innovations. First, a new provision distinguished between "soft" and "hard" drugs by means of two different ranges of penalties. A trafficker in soft drugs — usually cannabis products — could expect imprisonment ranging from one to six months. Those dealing in hard drugs — mainly heroin, cocaine and amphetamines — could expect a sentence ranging from six months to six years accompanied by a fine (Reeg, 1987:671). Taking into account the lesser danger arising from soft drugs, this distinction was seen by many as one of the major accomplishments of the reform.

A second important result of the 1983 reform was that mere possession of an illicit drug was removed from the list of punishable offenses. Only when possession was associated with trafficking did it remain punishable. Because of this, the courts had great difficulty determining under what circumstances possession was associated with trafficking and not with personal use. Aside from other factors such as determining whether an offender was a drug "addict" or in possession of precision scales or substances that could be used to adulterate the drug, the main point of distinction became the quantity of the drug found in possession at the time of arrest (Reeg, 1987:668-670).

The problem of distinguishing between possession for personal use and possession associated with trafficking led the Spanish Supreme Court to set up rebuttable presumptions in order to facilitate proof of an intention to traffic. For cannabis products a limit was drawn at 40 g (Reeg, 1987:669), and for heroin at 1.5 g (Spanish Supreme Court Sentence, 1986). Possession of these drugs in excess of these limits was considered to be for purposes of trafficking rather than personal use. Although the limits seemed to be rather clear, some legal uncertainty remained as to whether they referred to pure substances or to the mere weight of the seized drug regardless of purity.

Some major problems emerged after the Spanish Supreme Court held that the legal meaning of drug dealing covered all instances of distributing illicit drugs, even gratuitously, and regardless of the quantity involved (Spanish Supreme Court Sentence, 1983). Yet, notwithstanding these legal uncertainties, purchase and possession of any drug for personal use was statutorily exempt from punishment.

Third, apart from these basic elements of the offense, the 1983 reform introduced a number of statutorily qualified crimes that distinguished more clearly between the simple offense of drug trafficking and related activities considered more dangerous. Such activities were: (1) distribution of drugs to persons under 18 years of age, (2) committing the offense in an educational, military or penal institution, (3) trafficking in drugs as a member of a drug distribution organization, and (4) trafficking in quantities of "notorious importance."

While the first three of the above aggravated offenses did not present major difficulties of interpretation, the fourth one (trafficking in quantities of "notorious importance") involved the problem of determining or specifying the drug amount. For cannabis products a limit was fixed at about 1 kg (Spanish Supreme Court Sentence, 1985), and for heroin between 60 and 80 grams (Spanish Supreme Court Sentence, 1987). Once again, there was no clarification as to whether these amounts referred to the gross weight of the drug seized or only to its active component. This legal uncertainty was a crucial point in light of the different penalty ranges to be applied. A "normal" heroin trafficker was subject to six months to six years of imprisonment, whereas if the quantity involved was of "notorious importance," the range of penalties escalated to six to twelve years.

Apart from imprisonment, the 1983 reform provided a number of measures to deal with special aspects of certain narcotics offenses. Physicians involved in trafficking were suspended from medical practice. Companies or establishments involved in, or being the scene of, the commission of narcotics offenses were temporarily or permanently closed down.

On March 24, 1988, less than five years after the 1983 reform of the Criminal Drug Law, the Spanish government initiated another reform. It was widely felt that the previous legislation, including the 1983 revision, had proved to be insufficient and ineffective in combating the use of and traffic in illicit drugs (Ley Orgánica, 1988). The three main characteristics of the 1988 reform were: (1) an extension of punishable conduct included in the basic offense as well as a newly adopted list of aggravated cases, (2) a general increase in penalties, and (3) new legal powers to combat the increasing involvement of organized crime in drug trafficking (Muñoz Conde, 1988:447-466; Boix Reig, 1988:333-355; Rodríquez Devesa, *etc.*, 1988).

As far as the basic offense (Article 344 of the Penal Code) is concerned, the main difference compared to its predecessor is the considerably stiffer penalties. The distinction between hard and soft drugs has been maintained in the new law. When soft drugs are involved, prison terms range from four months to four years and two months, and fines from about US$4 250 to $425 000. Recall that in the 1983 revision, the penalty for trafficking in soft drugs was from one to six months' imprisonment. For hard drugs, the prison terms now range from two years and four months to eight years, and fines from US$8 500 to $850 000 (compared to the previous prison terms of six months to six years and much lower fines). This enormous increase in penalties is aimed at strengthening general prevention. In practice, the result is likely to be even more prisoners in Spain's already notoriously overcrowded jails. The new drug law also expands the notion of an aggravated offense contained in the 1983 reform. Consequently, supplying drugs to persons under the age of 18, in educational, military and correctional institutions, and to the mentally handicapped, is now seen as an aggravated offense. Aggravated offense also includes commission in establishments accessible to the public or by persons responsible for these establishments, the involvement of a "notoriously important" quantity of narcotics, supplying narcotics to people currently undergoing detoxification or drug rehabilitation, and adulterating or mixing drugs with substances in such a way as to endanger the user's health. In addition, aggravated offense occurs when the offender is part of an organization which is, even if only temporarily or occasionally, dedicated to the distribution of drugs. The penalities are higher if the offender holds a public post, or is a medical doctor, social worker, or educator.

From the viewpoint of legal policy, many of Spain's qualified offenses appear to make good sense. For instance, adulterating drugs or selling drugs to people undergoing detoxification would undoubtedly be seen by many as an aggravated offense. The problem is that the "solution" to such offenses is increased fines and extended imprisonment. For aggravated soft drug offenses, imprisonment can range from four years and two months to ten years, and fines can range from US$4 250 to about $640 000. When hard drugs are involved, imprisonment is from eight years to fourteen years and eight months, and fines from US$8500 to nearly $1.3 million.

Penalty ranges go one step further in a second group of aggravated cases (Article 344 bis [b] of the Penal Code) where they can reach up to twenty-three years and four months of imprisonment and fines of up to nearly US$2 million for hard drug cases. While it may be surprising that fines ranging up to US$2 million may be imposed in drug offense cases, an explanation can be found in Article 344 bis [d] of the Penal Code, which obliges the court to take into account the street value of the drugs in question and the offender's potential (though not actual) profits, when determining the fine. Such penalties are to be imposed in cases where the offenses are of "extreme severity" or when the offender is the head, manager, or commissioner of an organization principally engaged in the distribution of narcotics. The critical point, given the extreme sanctions, is the legal uncertainty as to what is meant by "cases of extreme severity." This wording gives rise to a considerable — some would say unacceptable — degree of judicial discretion, at least by European standards (Muñoz Conde, 1988:460).

Other important additions to the new law are increased measures to fight organized crime. These provisions are found in Article 344 bis [e] of the Penal Code, which permits the seizure and confiscation of vehicles, aircraft, and other items used in the commission of drug offenses, or which have been purchased from the proceeds of drug trafficking. Seizures are possible from the very start of criminal investigations.

Just as with the 1983 reform law, the 1988 provisions include a number of measures other than punishment to combat criminal organizations. These include the closure of businesses involved in trafficking (Article 344 bis [b] of the Penal Code). It is widely felt that, properly applied, such measures will have a deterrent effect on organized crime.

Another provision designed to combat organized crime deals with the offense (Article 546 bis [f] of the Penal Code) commonly known as "money laundering."[1] Until quite recently money laundering was not illegal in many countries. However, the United States has led the way in pointing out that criminal groups can be fought best by seizure of their assets. The 1988 revision specifically aims to help prosecutors trace the reinvestment of criminally gained profits derived from drug trafficking.

Finally, mention should be made of the new possibilities given by Article 93 bis of the Penal Code for probation orders pertaining to individuals committing offenses because of addiction to drugs. According to this article, probation orders are limited to cases in which conviction would ordinarily call for imprisonment not exceeding two years and where the defendant is not a recidivist. Given the high penalties described earlier, the benefit of probation may well apply to only a few offenders. Although this is definitely a point of criticism, the introduction of probation is certainly a departure from the tendency to rely on incarceration as the main means of control.

The 1988 reform also has some positive aspects. These include the maintenance of the distinction between soft and hard drugs, and the exemption of drug possession from punishment. It also gives the state increased power to counter organized drug trafficking. These include higher fines, seizure, confiscation and forfeiture of drug-related proceeds, as well as punishment for money laundering. Naturally these sanctions can be effective only when the procedural elements of prosecution work well. To this end, the Spanish government has established a new office of the Public Prosecutor specializing in narcotics crimes.

A number of points remain open to criticism. First, drug offenders are now subject to extremely high prison terms. If the experience of other countries is anything to go by, the imposition of long prison terms is a policy likely to result in failure (*Der Spiegel*, 1988). The only sense in which harsh punishments can be said to be positive is that they satisfy public demand. A second point of criticism is the treatment of user-traffickers who finance their addiction by dealing in small amounts of drugs. The law punishes these individuals as if they were full-time drug dealers. If one hopes to be able to encourage user-traffickers to return to a drug-free life, punishment is likely to be counterproductive. Finally, there is the legal ambiguity of determining what behavior constitutes an aggravated offense, which may lead to extremely high penalties (as much as 23 years' imprisonment). Depending on the discretion of the court, few or many offenses may be determined to be aggravated. As a result, drug offenses become a sort of "super offense" (Muñoz Conde, 1988:466) in the sense that the penalties may be disproportionate to the social harm they cause.

The 1988 reform of the 1983 Criminal Drug Law, or as the Spaniards call it, the "counter-reform," has not put an end to discussions on legal policies. In an effort to meet public demands, Spain is now considering the possibility of punishing the use of drugs consumed in public, a policy that can only be characterized as an expression of helplessness and a certain degree of public paranoia (*El País*, 1988u; *El País*, 1988w). Recourse to penal law is rarely the best way to deal with what is essentially a social problem, as was observed by von Liszt (1919) at the beginning of this century. Sharing this view are growing numbers of people, mainly specialists in the field of drug control policy, who are pushing for either liberalization or outright legalization of drug use in Spain.

Criminalization, Drug Profits, and Public Insecurity

As in other European countries, in Spain a heroin addict spends between US$150 to $400 in order to secure a daily supply of drugs. Unless an addict possesses an unusually high income, he or she will inevitably become involved in criminal activities to support this expensive habit. Therefore, addicts will steal, turn to prostitution, commit robberies and frauds, and even kill to get the money needed (*El País*, 1988u).[2] Public insecurity has thus become the top issue of the Spanish Home Affairs.

Drugs purchased in the street are often of poor quality and are nearly always adulterated in some manner. Sometimes an addict may happen upon a supply of unusually high-quality heroin and die as a result of overdose (*El País*, 1988i). Drug users also constantly run the risk of serious infection. In Spain, as elsewhere, criminalization of drug use makes it difficult for heroin users to acquire sterile needles and thereby lessen the danger of contracting AIDS.

There is an even more direct way in which criminalization affects the distribution and sale of illicit drugs: as government officials increase the suppression of the drug trade, the retail price of illicit drugs rises, along with the profits flowing to the drug dealers. Increased suppression opens opportunities for well-organized criminal networks to drive out competitors. These networks can also maintain effective distribution systems in the face of increased police pressure. As organized crime grows in power, its links with government and politicians strengthen. For example, the Bolivian drug trafficking organizations have offered to pay Bolivia's external debts in exchange for a freer rein. The Nicaraguan Contra rebels were largely financed by profits from drug trafficking (*El País*, 1988n). It has also been alleged that aircraft transporting U.S. weapons to Honduras often return from Central and South America loaded with narcotics (*Der Spiegel*, 1988:148-170). The involvement of General Manuel Noriega, Panama's ousted leader, in Latin American drug trafficking is known all over the world. Currently, US$50 billion is the rather conservative estimate of the value of the annual worldwide turnover from illicit drugs (*Der Spiegel*, 1988:3). Maintaining suppression through criminal law will only worsen this situation.

When we examine the effectiveness of the criminal prosecution of drug trafficking, the only fair conclusion is that it has failed. It is estimated that only 2% to 10% of the annual turnover in drugs can be seized (Serrano Gómez, 1986). Moreover, when drug seizures do increase, it does not necessarily prove that the police have become more effective. On the contrary, there is the distinct possibility that the drug trade has become even more active. Rather than being indicative of increased police effectiveness, spectacular drug seizures are often the result of rival criminal groups tipping off the police on one another's drug shipments in the hope of eliminating their competition (*Der Spiegel*, 1988:152).

Legalization as a Possible Solution

What, then, should be Spain's solution to its growing drug problem? Ever-increasing penalties? Liberalization or even legalization of drug dealing? Should Spain opt for a policy in which soft drugs can be sold under license and hard drugs sold under strict government controls? As in other parts of the world, a growing feeling prevails among those most familiar with the issues that the latter suggestions would indeed go some way in alleviating many of Spain's drug problems (*El País*, 1989b). Legalization would make it possible to reduce the staggering profits and debilitating political influence now enjoyed by drug-dealing criminals. It would allow addicts to live relatively normal lives by giving them an opportunity to escape from the vicious cycle of drugs-and-crime. It would also help protect them from contracting AIDS through sharing contaminated hypodermic needles. Some form of legalization might also work to lessen public insecurity. Legalization would enable the Spanish government to direct money now spent to finance criminal prosecution into public health information campaigns on the negative effects of drug use — including that of tobacco and alcohol. It would also be possible to tax the legalized drug trade as is already done in the Netherlands.

Spanish judges, police, and politicians have recently met to present ideas favoring the legalization of drugs (*El País*, 1988t). In addition, the Spanish Communist Party has recently campaigned for legalization (*El País*, 1988s). The push toward some form of legalization is hardly confined to Spain. In fact a drive towards legalization seems to be a common feature in many areas of the world that have heretofore relied upon a policy of criminalization. Marco Panella's Italian Radical Party, which has been quite successful in campaigning for similar issues, recently commenced a legalization campaign in Italy (*El País*, 1988r). The former West German Health Minister, Professor Sussmuth, has expressed support for legalization efforts in Germany (*Der Spiegel*, 1988:22-24). The Tilburg University Conference on Drug Policies in Western Europe in June 1988 recommended the elimination of criminal sanctions and the controlled distribution of drugs. It also specified drug trafficking as the only offense worth punishing — insofar as it violates individual liberty and harms the social order (*El País*, 1989c). One of the most recent steps in the direction of liberalized drug laws has been taken in Switzerland. As a result of a motion passed by Parliament, the government of the Canton of Berne, the Swiss capital, has asked the federal government to begin reforming the Swiss drug laws. Such reforms are to include: (1) reduction of punishable offenses to an indispensable minimum, (2) decriminalization of drug use (including the act of acquiring drugs), and (3) the possibility of mitigation of punishment for drug-addicted offenders (Berne Cantonal Government, 1988:3-4). In addition to these reforms, the possible legalization of soft drugs has also been mentioned. It remains to be seen if the Swiss will establish a growing trend in European drug law.

Notes

1. Money laundering "is the process by which one conceals the existence, illegal source, or illegal application of income, and then disguises that income to make it appear legitimate" (President's Commission on Organized Crime, 1984).

2. On November 12, 1988, a student who refused to give money to an addict who had asked him to do so was consequently killed by the addict with a knife.

References

Beristain Ipiña, Antonio. 1985. "Delitos de tráfico ilégal de drogas", in Manuel Cobo del Rosal (ed.), *Comentarios a la legislación penal*, pp. 743-810 Tomo V-Vol. 2. Madrid: EDERSA.

Berne Cantonal Government. 1988. Letter from the Berne Cantonal Government to the Swiss Federal Government. September 28, 1988.

Boix Reig, Javier. 1988. Tomás S. Vives Antón (ed.), *Derecho Penal, Parte Especial*, pp. 333-355. Second edition. Valencia: Tirant lo Blanch.

de la Cuesta Arzamendi, José Luis. 1988. "Spanish Drug Crime Policy." *Proceedings of the Conference on Drug Policies in Western Europe*. Tilburg University, Netherlands, May 30-June 2, 1988.

Dickey, Christopher. 1990. "The Porous South." *Newsweek* February 5:22-23.

Ley Orgánica. 1983. No. 8 of June 25, 1983.

———. 1988. No. 1 of March 24, 1988.

von Liszt, Franz. 1919. "Lehrbuch des deutschen Strafrechts" 21st and 22nd edition. Berlin: Guttentag.

Ministerio de Sanidad y Consumo. 1985. "Plan Nacional sobre drogas," p. 19, Madrid: Secretaría General Técnica, Servicio de Publicaciones.

Muñoz Conde, Francisco. 1988. "Derecho Penal, Parte Especial," pp. 447-466, 7th edition. Valencia: Tirant lo Blanch.

El País. 1987a. "Incautado en Barajas el mayor alijo de cocaína detectado en España." Madrid. September 30, 1987.

———. 1987b. "La sociedad española, preocupada e impotente ante el consumo de drogas." Madrid. October 16, 1987.

————. 1988a "La Guardia Civil captura en Barcelona un alijo de 562 kilos de cocaína, el mayor de España." Madrid. April 25, 1988.

————. 1988b. "El paro juvenil se acerca al 50% en la periferia urbana." Madrid. May 5, 1988.

————. 1988c. "Un agente de aduanas, implicado en la red que guardó 1000 kilos de cocaína en Irún." Madrid. May 9, 1988.

————. 1988d. "El juez toma declaración a los detenidos en relación con el alijo de 1000 kilos de cocaína." Madrid. May 11, 1988.

————. 1988e. "Tamames dice a la juez Carmena que al acusar a Yáñez de 'esnifar cocaína' denunciaba al PSOE." Madrid. May 17, 1988.

————. 1988f. "Petición de cuatro años de cárcel para un policía por tráfico de cocaína." Madrid. May 28, 1988.

————. 1988g. "Auger: 'Carecemos de justicia eficaz y de policía inteligente.'" Madrid. July 16, 1988.

————. 1988h. "Aprehendidas en la Costa Brava 17 toneladas de hachís." Madrid. July 26, 1988.

————. 1988i. "Una pureza que mata." Madrid. August 2, 1988.

————. 1988j. "Posible nexo del funcionario detenido con el narcotráfico." Madrid. August 3, 1988.

————. 1988k. "El paro en la CE disminuyó un 0.4% en junio." Madrid. August 9, 1988.

————. 1988l. "Los policías de Benidorm vinculados con drogas esperan la decisión judicial." Madrid. September 4, 1988.

————. 1988m. "El paro registrado descendió de nuevo en agosto, pero aún representa el 18, 79% la población activa." Madrid. September 13, 1988.

————. 1988n. "Cocaína para la Contra." Madrid. September 14, 1988.

————. 1988o. "La delincuencia aumentó en España un 8% el año pasado, según el fiscal general del Estado." Madrid. September 15, 1988.

————. 1988p. "Tamames, condenado a rectifar por no poder probar que Yáñez consuma droga." Madrid. September 17, 1988.

————. 1988q. "El Gobierno estima que el gasto público crecerá en 1989 tres veces más que el producto interior bruto." Madrid. September 17, 1988.

————. 1988r. "Los precios rebasan en 0.9 puntos el objetivo del gobierno cuatro meses antes de terminar el año." Madrid. September 20, 1988.

————. 1988s. "Panella, contra la prohibición de las drogas." Madrid. September 22, 1988.

————. 1988t. "El PCE propone una política contra la droga basada en la legislación controlada." Madrid. September 28, 1988.

————. 1988u. "Jueces, policías, políticos y expertos piden la legislación de la droga." Madrid. October 28, 1988.

————. 1988v. "Diversos juristas españoles plantean la despenalización del tráfico de drogas." Madrid. November 14, 1988.

―――. 1988w. "El asesinato de un estudiante por unos 'rockers' aumenta las críticas vecinales por la 'degradación' Chamberí." Madrid. November 14, 1988.

―――. 1988x. "Las empresas españolas cuadruplican sus beneficios en dos años." Madrid. November 16, 1988.

―――. 1988y. "A golpe de Código." Madrid. November 17, 1988.

―――. 1988z. "Los 'ertzainas' detenidos con droga dirigían una red de traficantes." Madrid. November 21, 1988.

―――. 1989a. "La ira de los ciudadanos." Madrid. October 4, 1989.

―――. 1989b. "La legalización de la droga, una medida controvertida que va ganando lentamente adeptos." Madrid. August 10, 1989.

―――. 1989c. "Tomarse libertades." Madrid. October 25, 1989.

El País Domingo. 1988a. "En bandeja de plata." Madrid. Año 4, No. 162. November 20, 1988.

―――. 1988b. "Tabaco." Madrid. Año 4, No. 162. November 20, 1988.

President's Commission on Organized Crime. 1984. *The Cash Connection: Organized Crime, Financial Institutions, and Money Laundering.* Washington, D.C.: U.S. Government Printing Office.

Reeg, Axel R. 1987. "Landesbericht Spanien", pp. 653-727, in Jürgen Meyer (ed.), *Betäubungsmittelstrafrecht in Westeuropa.* Freiburg: Max-Planck-Institut für Strafrecht.

Serrano Gómez, Alfonso. 1983. *Evolución Social, Criminalidad y Cambio Político en España.* Madrid: Anuario de Derecho Penal y Ciencias Penales.

―――. 1986. "El costo del delito y sus víctimas en España." Madrid: UNED.

―――. 1988. Rodríquez Devesa, José María and Alfonso Serrano Gómez (eds.). *Derecho Penal Español, Parte Especial*, pp. 1068-1087. Eleventh Edition. Madrid: Dyckinson.

Spanish Supreme Court Sentence (STS). 1983. R.A. (Aranzadi, Repertorio de Jurisprudencia) No. 6716 of December 21, 1983.

―――. 1985. R.A. No. 6352 of December 20, 1985.

―――. 1986. R.A. No. 4059 of July 9, 1986 .

―――. 1987. La Ley 1987-3, No. 304 of May 5.

Der Spiegel. 1988. "Weltmacht Droge." Hamburg. November 7, 1988.

Süeddeutsche Zeitung. 1988a. "Über der iberischen Halbinsel strahlt die Sonne." Munich. No. 199. August 30, 1988.

―――. 1988b. "Berner Regierung will Drogenkonsum freigeben." Munich. No. 230. October 5, 1988.

4

Finnish Drug Control: Change and Accommodation

Ahti Laitinen

In many parts of the world illegal drug trafficking is a major industry. According to some estimates the cocaine trade in the United States exceeds Finland's annual state budget by 500%. In certain Latin American countries, such powerful drug trafficking organizations exist that government resistance to them is severely emasculated (Garreau, 1982; Määttänen, 1988).

In the Nordic countries, the situation is very different. Nordic countries have a distinctive culture, despite their obvious connections to other European nations. One of their features is the policy goal of guaranteeing the best possible social welfare for all citizens. Consequently, real poverty in Scandinavia is unusual. Another feature of the Nordic countries is that, except in Denmark, official attitudes on alcohol use have been severe. The alcohol industry is a state monopoly and the price level is kept intentionally high. This cultural attitude towards alcohol also applies to drug policy.

The population of the Scandinavian countries is small. Even Sweden, the largest country in the region, has a population of only 8.3 million. On the other hand, the land areas of Sweden, Finland and Norway are the largest in Europe next to the Commonwealth of Independent States, France, and Spain. Thus the population density of the region is also very low. In Scandinavia there are only two large cities comparable to those in Europe: Stockholm and Copenhagen. It follows that social problems linked to high population density and large urban areas are not very significant in the Nordic countries.

Geographically, linguistically, and, in part, culturally, these countries have been somewhat isolated from the other European countries. In Finland this has been reinforced up to the present by its isolationist foreign policy.[1] Another distinguishing feature of Finland is that industrialization has come late. These facts partly explain why Scandinavia has been relatively immune from social problems prevalent in the rest of the continent. Nevertheless, the present fact is that the Nordic countries (in spite of Finland and Sweden's neutrality) are rapidly becoming integrated with the European Community (E.C.) and are adjusting their economic and social policies with those of the E.C. countries. These changes have caused questions to be raised in the Nordic countries about what they portend for drug use in the future.

In light of these impending changes and the debate they have fostered, I will analyze (1) drug legislation in Finland and other Nordic countries, (2) the scope of drug use — consumption, importation, physical harm, and offense patterns — in Scandinavia, (3) the organization of the drug trade within the region, and (4) Nordic drug policy.

Drug Legislation in Finland

The concept of illegal drugs has been defined in the Nordic countries in a Western framework and, in general, is based on international agreements. Prior to the 1960s, Finland was somewhat reluctant to develop a national drug policy although already a signatory to some international agreements.

The 1960s saw the first signs of the spread of hashish to Finland. As a result, special units to confront this were established by the police. The use of drugs (except for medical purposes) was criminalized in 1966 through an amendment to a Finnish decree (Nr 514/1966.)[2] Criminalization was put on a higher statutory level by the passing of the 1972 Narcotics Act (Nr 41/1972). Besides Finland, the only Western European countries that have criminalized the use of narcotics are Norway and Greece. Criminalization of *use* makes it possible to arrest suspects and carry out searches of their premises for even minor offenses. However, production, sale, and possession of drugs are crimes in all Nordic countries.

A new Narcotics Decree was passed in Finland in 1981. A large number of medical substances, particularly psychoactive drugs, were criminalized (again, except for actual medicinal use). The intensification of official control at this time was not connected with international agreements, as it was not until 1984 that the United Nations Commission of Narcotics, following a close vote, included psychoactive drugs in its list of narcotics. (For a more detailed history of Finnish drug legislation, see Utriainen and Hakonen, 1985.)

Drug Use in Finland and Other Nordic Countries

Consumption.   It is impossible to provide precise figures showing the frequency of illegal drug consumption, although there are some studies concerning the casual use of drugs among young men between the ages of 19 and 21 (Nordic Working Group, 1984; Christie and Bruun, 1986:113). As in North America and elsewhere in Europe, the most commonly used drugs have been cannabis products, and an estimated 10% to 20% of young people (under age 30) have tried these substances. The number of regular users, of course, is much lower. In Finland, for example, it is estimated that less than 1% of the population falls within this category. According to various studies, the number of drug users in Sweden is estimated to be between 10 000 and 14 000, or one-fifth of 1% of the total population. Corresponding numbers for Denmark and Norway are 6000 to 10 000, and 3000 to 4500, respectively. The figures for Finland are believed to be even lower (Virolainen, 1985:36-41; Christie and Bruun, 1986:111-121; Kontula, 1987:58-61).

Importation.   Another means of studying the extent of drug use is to analyze the amount of confiscated narcotics. It is clear, of course, that the amount confiscated is only a small part of the total amount imported. Police and other state officials in the Nordic countries work closely in trying to prevent importation of illegal drugs into Scandinavia, and this helps explain why the figures of the Nordic countries are similar.

Relative to other European countries, the confiscation amounts in Finland, Norway, and Sweden are low. Nevertheless, in recent years customs officers have made some relatively large-scale confiscations at Finland's Helsinki airport. Finnish law enforcement officials have assumed that the seized drugs were intended for the markets of other European countries. But, of course, this can be no more than an assumption.

Except in Denmark where it is permissible to plant poppies (but not for the production of opiates) and hemp (for the production of cannabis for personal use), private drug production is prohibited within Scandinavia.

Physical harm. The number of deaths caused by illegal drugs has been low in the Scandinavian countries. On the basis of various studies, the figures for Denmark (population 5 million) have been a bit lower than 150 per year throughout the 1980s. In Norway (population 4 million) the annual figures varied between 20 and 45 during the early 1980s. In Finland (population 5 million), the annual number of deaths caused by illegal drugs has been approximately 300 per year. These figures also include suicides involving illegal drugs as well as deaths caused by the medical use of drugs. In Sweden (population 8 million), 40 to 50 deaths were caused annually by drugs in the early 1980s, but these figures may now be two or three times higher (Christie and Bruun, 1986:172-177). All these deaths are a terrible waste, of course, but, to be realistic, it is necessary to compare these figures with other fatality statistics, such as homicides, traffic accidents, and cirrhosis of the liver.

Table 1 Some Causes of Death in Nordic Countries in 1987–89[1]

	Motor vehicle traffic accident			Homicide and other injuries			Cirrhosis of liver		
Country	1987	1988	1989	1987	1988	1989	1987	1988	1989
Denmark	678	712	641	54	57	62	701	658	726
Finland	537	649	–	133	138	–	423	480	–
Norway	405	363	–	60	50	–	318	280	–
Sweden	764	–	–	101	–	–	612	–	–

(Year Book of Nordic Statistics 1988 and 1990)
[1]Year Book of Nordic Statistics, 1991 does not include "causes of death."

Table 1 shows that illegal drugs are not a very significant cause of death in the Nordic countries. Moreover, while traffic accidents and cirrhosis of the liver are usually defined as "natural" causes of death, those due to illegal drugs are more apt to be defined as "unnatural" and therefore somehow threatening to society.

Drug offenses. A fourth means of describing the scope of drug use is that of analyzing the number of arrests for drug offenses. A comparison to the other Nordic countries shows that the figures for Finland are the lowest. The figures for Finland are only 10% of those for Sweden, 15% of those for Denmark, and 50% of those for Norway. In addition, it appears that the offenses detected in Finland are, on the average, less serious than in the other Nordic countries.

Finnish drug offenses are classified according to their "seriousness." The most essential criterion for assessing seriousness has been the amount of the drug. Drug cases are considered to be "aggravated" if there is evidence to suggest they are part of an ongoing business enterprise. In the case of hashish, for example, the distinction between aggravated and routine offenses varied from 800 g to 1000 g during the 1970s. During the 1980s, 500 g constituted an aggravated case, and most recently the amount was again increased to about 1 kg. For heroin, the line has varied from a "few" grams to 20 g.[3] The share of narcotics offenses classified as

Table 2 Number of Persons Convicted for Narcotic Offenses in Finland

Year	Aggravated offenses[1]	Other offenses	Total
1972	27	570	597
1973	15	572	587
1974	50	586	618
1975	36	569	605
1976	37	437	474
1977	25	436	461
1978	37	430	467
1979	12	531	543
1980	19	430	449
1981	21	348	369
1982	16	624	640
1983	31	788	819
1984	40	882	922
1985	69	928	997
1986	45	885	930
1987	44	816	860

(National Institute of Legal Policy, 1990)
[1]Includes "smuggling of narcotics."

aggravated has averaged about 5%. This indicates that often the amount of drugs has not been large. The most typical narcotics offense in Finland has been "the use, possession, and purchase" of cannabis products.

The most reliable information on Finnish drug offenses is published by the courts. The number of persons sentenced for drug offenses in Finland was 860 in 1987 (see Table 2). Compared to the number of persons sentenced for alcohol offenses, the amount is less than one-tenth. On the other hand, the punishments for drug offenses have been much more severe. There were 210 prison sentences in 1987 for drug offenses, but only 123 for alcohol offenses.

Between 1972 and 1981, the number of detected drug cases in Finland declined. In 1981 there were only 400 drug cases brought to court. Moreover, the average age of persons accused of drug offenses has shown a significant change since the early 1970s. Previously drug offenses were a typical aspect of juvenile delinquency. Nowadays they are crimes of adults. The average age of those brought to trial during this period increased from 18.5 to almost 25. While the proportion of women among the accused has remained at about one-fifth throughout the period in question, their average age has been somewhat below that of men. The proportion of foreigners (tourists) among those brought to court has remained below 5%.

After 1981, the number of drug offenses in Finland again began to increase. The latest statistics show a small increase in the number of drug offenses; for years 1984, 1985, and 1986 — the figures being 922, 997, and 930, respectively (National Institute of Legal Policy, 1988). According to police statistics, the number of narcotics offenses at present is similar to that in the 1970s. During the 1980s the detected offenses have been committed during previous years. That is, a relatively greater number of "old" offenses have emerged during police investigations. The effectiveness of police investigations is also reflected in the fact that drugs have been confiscated from only one in four of those suspected for drug offenses. In three out of four cases, evidence is secured through other means, primarily through questioning of suspected persons in connection with arrests (Kontula, 1987:55-58.)

Compared to other Western European countries, the time between arrest and trial in Finland until 1989 was very long, averaging nearly 21 days. That figure has been reduced to only four

Table 3   Percentage Contribution That Different Drugs Make to Drug Offenses Known to the Police.

Year	Cannabis	Legal drugs	Amphetamine	Opiates	Others
1968–1984	77	7	6	5	6
1985	63	15	11	5	5
1986	73	13	11	2	1
1987	67	19	11	2	1
1988	64	19	14	3	0
1989	60	23	14	2	1
1990	57	27	14	1	1

(National Institute of Legal Policy, 1990, 1991)

days now. According to the police, the longer pre-trial periods before 1989 made it easier to investigate crimes. Nevertheless, in Finland the shortening of this time has been given higher priority as a matter of humanitarian concern.

Table 3 shows the relative proportions of different drug offenses known to the police. Each offense has been registered only once, according to the more serious drug in those cases where several drugs have been used. It is clear that the share of cannabis offenses has been at least two-thirds throughout the period 1968 to 1984.

According to Table 4, a large majority of drug offenses in Finland entail the use, possession, and purchase of illegal drugs. Approximately two-thirds of the offenses involve the use or possession of relatively small amounts for personal use. Smuggling and selling drugs, which have mostly involved transporting and acting as an intermediary, account for about 30% of total drug offenses.

Table 4   Percentage Distributions of Different Types of Narcotic offenses in Finland, 1973–1990.

Content of the offence	1973–1984 on average	1985	1986	1987	1988	1989	1990
Use	53	39	45	45	43	41	30
Possession	17	9	11	10	14	21	33
Sale	12	15	14	14	11	13	9
Delivering	5	9	8	6	3	3	4
Transferring	5	5	3	3	2	3	2
Smuggling	7	12	13	15	18	10	8
Others	4	11	6	7	9	9	14

(National Institute of Legal Policy, 1990, 1991)

When drugs are in short supply, leading to an increase in price, some users are forced to obtain money illegally. So far this supplementary criminal activity seems fairly uncommon among those found guilty of drug offenses in Finland. Over the past few years, an average of 15% of offenders brought to court on these charges have also had other charges facing them. Only one-half of these additional charges have been for property crimes. It can therefore be said that less than one-tenth of those charged with a drug offense have also been charged with a property offense.

Approximately 70% of drug cases brought to court in Finland lead to fines. Unconditional and conditional sentences of imprisonment each account for a further 10%. Among remaining cases, punishment is either waived or the accused found not guilty. On the basis of the 72 cases selected for analysis from the records of the Helsinki City Court, those who have been fined have generally used a maximum of 20 g of hashish, or have transferred or sold very small amounts to their friends (Kontula, 1986:256). As the proportion of fines is so large, it seems obvious that most narcotics offenses in Finland involve small amounts of hashish.

The incomes of persons convicted of drug offenses is generally very low. The amount of "day-fines" depends on the income of the defendant.[4] Recently the minimum day-fine has been about US$5, based on a maximum monthly income of around US$450. The proportion of those with low incomes sentenced in 1987 was more than two-thirds of all those sentenced for drug offenses.

Regionally, drug offenses have been concentrated within Helsinki and other cities along the coast. In 1988, 89% of the drug offenses known to the police took place in cities — 48% in the Helsinki area alone — and 30% in other parts of southern Finland.

Is the Drug Trade Organized in the Nordic Countries?

In many parts of the world — Colombia, Japan, and Southeast Asia, for example — the drug trade is organized and powerful. The economies of some Caribbean and Latin American countries are heavily dependent on the drug trade. In North America and Europe, criminal organizations are deeply embedded within local and national political and economic structures (Chambliss, 1988a).

In the Nordic countries as well, it is commonly believed there are powerful "drug barons" who entice youth into becoming illegal drug users. Yet, according to Bodal (1982), there is little evidence of organized drug trafficking in Norway. His findings show that, between 1968 and 1980, persons convicted of drug offenses were seeminly ordinary citizens or criminals from poor social backgrounds (Christie and Bruun, 1985:99-101).[5] Persson (1982) reports from Sweden that the belief that the incomes of drug offenders are exceptionally high is totally without foundation. Other Swedish researchers have calculated average incomes, and the conclusions are that the money derived from drug trafficking is too little to indicate the existence of any well-organized enterprises (Christie and Bruun, 1985:102). In Finland, Kontula (1986) has studied the most important drug cases handled by the courts in recent years. He has found some evidence of low-level organization, but nothing approaching what is ordinarily meant by "organized crime." The members of these "organizations" were mainly young people, most of whom were unemployed and from poor social backgrounds.

It is possible, of course, to argue that the authorities have yet to identify the leaders of Scandinavia's major drug organizations. While it may be assumed that the drug trade within Scandinavia is more considerable than is revealed by official statistics, available data concerning the confiscation and smuggling of drugs within the region do not support the existence of heretofore undiscovered major drug traffickers. There is simply no credible evidence of a well-organized and professional drug trade in the Nordic region.

Drug Policy in the Nordic Countries

Drug and alcohol control policies are linked with each other in a number of aspects. There are, for example, signs that the liberalization of alcohol policy enables official attention to shift to illegal drugs. At present there are pressures to change Nordic alcohol policy to become more in line with European-wide policies. If and when these liberal changes occur, they could lead to tighter control over drugs and especially over drug users.

If the most important goal of any sensible drug policy is the control of international trafficking, then more attention should be paid to control the drug trade as a business enterpise rather than to control individual users (Haller, 1990). One element of this policy might be to legalize the use of some currently illegal drugs. Simultaneous pressures to liberalize alcohol might, however, be too much change for a conservative society like Finland to accept. Thus the linkage of drug and alcohol policies could become an obstacle to developing a more reasonable drug policy.

The factors of sex, age, financial status, and life-style of drug offenders have also been studied. Women account for only one-fifth of known drug offenders. It would appear that the use of illegal drugs by women comes to the attention of the police primarily when a husband or male companion is apprehended. Those responsible for the control of drugs in Finland would seem to be less interested in women's use of drugs. The same observation has been made regarding Sweden (Rexed and Sesser, 1981). In addition, women receive lighter sentences for the same offenses, and the periods for which they are placed under arrest are shorter. The main reason for this is that women are apparently considered less responsible for their offenses than men (Kontula, 1987).

Drug control in Finland is directed primarily towards males, especially young ones, while drug use committed by middle-aged women draws virtually no official concern. The authorities are particularly interested in young people who frequent public places and live an "irregular life." Of those sentenced to fines in Finland for drug law violations, fully one-half are without income, and only a few earn an amount that is average for the population (Kontula, 1987:63-64).

Christie and Bruun (1986) have strongly criticized the drug policy in the Nordic countries. First, legal control, with respect to possession and use of drugs, is exerted principally against young users, and official policy has ignored the social conditions which form the background of young drug users. This oversight is remarkable, because this group is one of the weakest in Nordic society.

Second, when comparing the various forms of harm caused to society by crime, it is clear that the harm caused by drug use is relatively small. Yet government expenditure for drug control is substantial compared to that targeting other forms of criminality. Cristie and Bruun's explanation for the disproportionate emphasis on drugs is that society requires a scapegoat for its shortcomings, a need nicely satisfied by the relatively weak and powerless drug user.

Similar situations exist elsewhere. It is more convenient for police to attack highly visible street-level drug users than the underlying economic and political factors. In another context, Cullen, Maakestad, and Cavender (1987:321) have presented the example of former U.S.

President Carter's efforts to target U.S. corporate and white-collar crime. Nevertheless, this policy was such a potential threat to the economic and political elites of American society that it was soon abandoned. Soon after assuming office in 1981, President Reagan moved quickly to restore blue-collar "street crime" and especially drug trafficking as the Justice Department's foremost priorities.

Third, the attempt to prohibit drug use completely in the Nordic countries is impractical. Christie and Bruun (1986) suggest it might be worthwhile to decriminalize the use of cannabis products. The same suggestion has been made by a high-ranking Finnish legislator who argues that the police are not the appropriate authorities to deal with the problems of drug users (Seppälä, 1987).

In Finland, a society called "Narcotics Free" was established in 1983. This organization came into being because its founders believed drug policy ignored the care and resocialization of young drug users. "Narcotics Free" suggested, as one improvement, the adoption of a system of coercive treatment. The group's members worry mainly about the future of young drug users — often their own children. Nevertheless, state officials argue that such means are unacceptable in a democratic society.

While movements such as "Narcotics Free" are mainly interested in drug use insofar as it damages those most vulnerable, such as the young, Finnish government officials are mainly interested in drug use as criminality. Can the drug problem be solved by either means? Nordic examples show that the answer is "no." While coercive drug "treatment" might relieve the suffering of drug users and their families, and repressive police measures may temporarily deter street-level drug use, the basic underlying social conflicts will remain unresolved (Chambliss, 1988b).

Conclusion

Compared to other European countries, the use of illegal drugs in Finland and the other Nordic countries is slight, and to a large degree limited to cannabis. There is no credible evidence that Scandinavian criminal organizations are involved in illegal drug trafficking. Nevertheless, the forthcoming political and economic integration of Europe will foster increased commercial activity between member countries, and it is possible that criminal organizations elsewhere in the European Community will try to expand their reach to the Nordic area.

Scandinavian governments have attempted tighter control of illegal drugs in the past decade. The principal policies, however, have been to impose increasingly severe punishments and to focus law enforcement on youthful offenders. Official policy has been relatively unconcerned with prevention, treatment, or resocialization. For the most part, private aid organizations established to meet these needs have had limited success due to lack of funds and often strained relations with government officials.

While many Scandinavian observers acknowledge that the present situation is not alarming, who knows what the future will bring? The Nordic countries cannot help but fear possible threats to their national integrity. For a long time Finns believed they were so isolated that the international drug problem would never affect them. But recently, due to Finnish bank secrecy laws, some problems have emerged within the banking industry which are indeed troubling. Due, in part, to the ease of opening bank accounts without fear of police investigation, Finnish banks offer international drug dealers the opportunity to launder drug money.

Though money laundering itself is not illegal in Finland, a few accounts opened in Finnish banks were "frozen" by the police in 1989. This was possible only because the police had incontrovertible evidence that the deposits were directly related to drug crimes. The Central Criminal Police suspect millions of dollars in drug money have been deposited in Finland's banks, but no one outside the banking industry knows whether or not such deposits actually exist. In the meantime, Finnish authorities are waiting for a forthcoming E.C. directive concerning the investigation of banks within member countries suspected of laundering drug money. Finnish authorities have made clear they will ratify the agreement in 1992.

The creation of a "drug free" world is an unrealistic concept. The aim, therefore, must be to reduce the various costs, both for individual drug users and society at large. Any humane and realistic drug policy must be framed in such a way that drug users are spared from additional damage at the hands of state control (Jepsen, 1988:30). A useful first step in this direction would be to decriminalize the use of drugs. This would be immediately helpful to drug users, and in the longer run would drive organized crime out of the market.

Notes

1. In recent years the Finnish government has been most restrictive in its willingness to accept more than a few dozen refugees and other immigrants annually, and even then only from certain countries. During the early 1970s, the majority of immigrants came from Chile; in the latter half of the decade most were Vietnamese. In the past two years immigrants have been accepted from Africa and certain Eastern European countries. Russian dissidents stood virtually no chance of being granted political asylum in Finland.

2. This decree can be found in the Finnish Collection of Laws and Administrative Orders.

3. Because there are no precise limits mentioned in the law, the courts must consider this matter, as well as other criteria, when defining an offense as aggravated. According to *Rikollisuustilanne (Criminality in Finland)* the amount is simply stated as "a few" grams. On the other hand, Kontula (1986) and Utriainen and Hakonen (1985) mention ten grams as the customary minimum amount of heroin. However, *Rikollisuustilanne* (National Institute of Legal Policy, 1988) is the more recent publication.

4. Finland is among a number of countries with a system of fines called "day-fines." One day-fine is equal to a person's monthly income divided by 90. I have mentioned the minimum amount of one day-fine. The present figure was established in the Decree of Day-Fines (Nr 786/1985). During the 1980s, the median number of day-fines for drug offenses was 20.1 (National Institute of Legal Policy, 1988:76).

5. In Norway and Finland, according to national police statistics, studies referred to here, and the *Rikollisuustilanne* (National Institute of Legal Policy, 1988), almost all persons convicted of drug offenses are of such a poverty level that the probability they have been the organizers or members of organized "criminal drug networks" is virtually nil. In 1989, a young Finnish man was sentenced to eight years' imprisonment for having masterminded such an organization. The "organization" was so small, however, that after his arrest it completely dissolved.

References

Bodal, Kare. 1982. *350 narkoslegere.* Oslo: Universiteitsforlaget (Norwegian University Press).

Chambliss, William J. 1988a. *On the Take: From Petty Crooks to Presidents.* Rev. Ed. Bloomington: Indiana University Press.

———. 1988b. *Exploring Criminology.* New York: Macmillan.

Christie, Nils and Kettil Bruun. 1986. *Hyvä vihohollinen.* Espoo, Finland: Weilin and Goos.

Cullen, Francis T., William J. Maakestad and Gray Cavender. 1987. *Corporate*

Crime Under Attack: The Ford Pinto Case and Beyond. Cincinnati: Anderson.

Garreau, Joel. 1982. *The Nine Nations of North America.* New York: Avon Books.

Haller, Mark H. 1990. "Ilegal Enterprise: A Theoretical and Historical Interpretation." *Criminology* 28:207-235.

Jepsen, Jørgen. 1988. "Drug Policies in Denmark," paper presented at the Conference on Drug Policies in Western Europe. Tilburg, Netherlands: Katholike Universiteit.

Kontula, Osmo. 1986. *Huumausainerikokset ja niiden kontrolli: Tilanne Suomessa 1960-luvulta 1980-luvulle,* Publication No. 76, National Research Institute of Legal Policy, Helsinki.

————. 1987 "Special Features of Narcotics Control and the Narcotics Situation in Finland," in Per Strangeland (ed.), *Drugs and Drug Control in Scandinavia, Scandinavian Studies in Criminology,* Vol. 8. Oslo: Norwegian University Press/Oxford University Press.

Määttänen, Sakari. 1988. Se sota on jo hävitty. *Helsingin Sanomat,* May 15.

National Institute of Legal Policy. 1988. *Rikollisuustilanne 1987.* Helsinki: National Research Institute of Legal Policy.

————. 1990. *Rikollisuustilanne 1989.* Helsinki: National Research Institute of Legal Policy.

————. 1991. *Rikollisuustilanne 1990.* Helsinki: National Research Institute of Legal Policy.

Nordic Statistical Secretariat. 1988. *Yearbook of Nordic Statistics* Vol. 27. Stockholm: Nordic Council of Ministers and the Nordic Statistical Secretariat.

————. 1990. *Yearbook of Nordic Statistics* Vol. 28. Stockholm: Nordic Council of Ministers and the Nordic Statistical Secretariat.

————. 1991. *Yearbook of Nordic Statistics* Vol. 29. Stockholm: Nordic Council of Ministers and the Nordic Statistical Secretariat.

Nordic Working Group. 1984. Narkotikasituationen i Norden: Rapport från en nordisk arbetsgrupp till kontakmannaorganet för narkotika frågor. January.

Persson, Leif. 1982. "Knarkpolisens rövarromantik har tagit över verkilgheten." *Dagens Nyheter* April 28.

Rexed, Ingemar and Marie Sesser. 1981. Narkotikaligor. *Nordisk Tidsskrift för kriminalvidenskab* 68:106-119.

Seppälä, Heikk. 1987. "Huumausaineiden kaytosta ei tulisi rangaista." *Helsingin Sanomat,* November 12.

Utriainen, Terttu and Kimmo Hakonen (eds.). 1985. *Huumausainerikokset.* Mänttä: Suomen Lakimiesliiton Kustannus Oy.

Virolainen, Pertti. 1985. "Huumausainerikollisuus poliisin kannalta." In *Huumeetko ongelmana Suomessa?,* Veikko J. Valkonen et al. (eds.). Helsinki: Vakuutusyhtioiden Tiedotuskeskus.

Part II ━━━━━━━━━━━━

The Political Economy of Drugs

5

The Chinese Laundry: International Drug Trafficking and Hong Kong's Banking Industry

Mark S. Gaylord

For mainland Chinese with hopes of relocating eventually in the West, Hong Kong has long been a way station. The British colony's transient population has been made up mostly of Cantonese, those who originate from the region around the city of Guangzhou (Canton) just north of Hong Kong, and it is the Cantonese whose language and culture dominate in the city.

Part of this cultural heritage involves an organized crime tradition that dates back nearly a hundred years. Triad "secret societies" were originally part of a patriotic resistance movement on the part of ethnic Chinese in protest to the political domination by Manchu rulers from the North who had overthrown the Ming rulers in 1644 and formed the Ching Dynasty (Crowell and Tsang, 1988). Throughout the long years, Triad members were respected for their fighting courage, fierce in-group loyalty and nationalistic fervor. Years later, when Dr. Sun Yat Sen established the Chinese Republic, the Triads came forth to help him. However, after 1912 most of the Triads degenerated into little more than criminal bands. In his bid to control China, Sun's successor, Chiang Kai Shek, repeatedly turned to the Triads, which by then had become largely an unlawful horde with heavy involvement in the

Much of this chapter originally appeared in Mark S. Gaylord, "The Chinese Laundry: International Drug Trafficking and Hong Kong's Banking Industry," *Contemporary Crises* 14 (March, 1990):23-37.

opium trade. In fact, Chiang, as Dr. Sun before him, was himself a Triad member, and relied so heavily on his Triad allies that they served as generals, soldiers, spies, businessmen, and hired thugs in his Kuomintang, the Chinese Nationalist Party (Seagrave, 1985). After the successful Communist Revolution in the late 1940s, the Triads were virtually eliminated in the People's Republic of China. Drug dealers were rounded up and imprisoned; many were summarily executed by the simple expedient of a bullet to the back of the head. Today it is generally agreed that the Communist Revolution ended China's long nightmare with opium addiction. It did not, however, put an end to the Triads. Wherever Chiang's army fled, the Triads went along — to Hong Kong and Taiwan, and from the south of China into the Golden Triangle and other parts of Southeast Asia where they have since flourished (Kaplan, Goldberg, and Jue, 1986).

Even before 1949, in part due to the policies pursued by the Japanese during World War II, Hong Kong had already confronted serious problems with Triad gangs. After falling to Japan during the war, the colony's new masters organized co-operative Triads into the Hing Ah Kee Kwan, the "Asia Flourishing Society," and used them to help keep order. The Japanese shared with their collaborators the profits from prostitution and gambling, and gave the gangs control of the opium trade throughout the colony (Crisswell and Watson, 1982). The occupying Japanese, as the British before them, relied heavily on opium addiction to keep the population docile (Block and Chambliss, 1981).

After the war, and with Hong Kong once again in British hands, the Triads extended their influence within the colony, aided by the massive influx of fellow members fleeing the mainland. Throughout the first decade after the war, the British viewed the Triads as useful in helping to integrate the huge rush of refugees into Hong Kong society. However, this same period saw the British make the "grave mistake" (Dubro and Kaplan, 1986) of banning opium in the colony. It was an error which immediately gave rise to a thriving black market and a steady source of income for the postwar gangs. Soon the local Triads were playing a central role in the world's narcotics trade. Today the Hong Kong-Chinese syndicates are said to play a key role in smuggling almost half the heroin reaching the West Coast of the United States (Camens, 1988). Some American law enforcement officials are convinced that Chinese syndicates form a major multinational link in organized crime today (Kerr, 1988).

The Golden Triangle

Hong Kong's Triads have grown in part because of the city's proximity to the Golden Triangle. The vast majority of Southeast Asian heroin controlled by Hong Kong's drug syndicates originates in that fabled region where Burma, Laos, and Thailand meet in a borderless land of hill tribes and medieval warlords. In this no-man's region begins a long, tortuous route of opium production, refining and smuggling that ultimately supplies the U.S., Australia, Canada, the U.K., and the Netherlands.

The opium poppy requires an environment that combines a warm climate and high altitude. This combination is found in the chain of mountains that extends from Turkey through Iran, India, China, and Southeast Asia. However, no more favorable place in all the world is to be found for growing opium poppies than deep within the Golden Triangle, in the Shan and Kachin States pocketed in the rugged mountains of northern Burma. Geographically the Golden Triangle is bounded by the Mae Sai and Mekong rivers, creating a virtually un-policed territory about the size of England. It is a place of breathtakingly beautiful mountains covered by dense, green jungles. Within it there are few paths, and even fewer roads. However, the hill tribes people who grow the opium poppies — the Shan, the Hmong, the Wa, and the Ahka — know how to traverse this seemingly impassable terrain with apparent ease (Freemantle, 1985).

Despite concerted international efforts to halt the drug traffic, and the expenditure of more than US$98 million of related American assistance since 1972, the Golden Triangle remains today the source of up to 40% of the heroin entering the West Coast of the United States and between 80% and 90% of the heroin entering the world's largest heroin market, New York City (Dear, 1988). Although vast quantities of the drug are now produced in Mexico and Southwest Asia's "Golden Crescent" — Iran, Afghanistan, Pakistan, and India — many of America's narcotics dealers continue to prefer the generally higher quality of Golden Triangle heroin (Dubro and Kaplan, 1986).

It is at the point of refining the heroin that the 16 000-member Chiu Chao Triads first come into play. Their skilled "chemists," often imported from Hong Kong or Macau, oversee production as the opium sap is first processed into morphine, and then bonded with acetic anhydride to produce 99%-pure, No. 4 heroin. Generally acknowledged to be the most tightly organized of the numerous Triad societies, the Chiu Chao took control of heroin distribution in Thailand in the 1950s. Together with their brothers in Hong Kong, the Thai Chiu Chao finance billions of dollars in heroin shipments worldwide. Their many deals over the years with the Corsican, Sicilian, Japanese, and American drug syndicates have earned them the reputation as the Mafia of the Chinese underworld (McCoy, 1972; Block, and Chambliss, 1981). Today, however, their dominance is less secure. Along with the Kejia, Fujianese and Hong Kong Cantonese, the Chiu Chao are joined in a high-stakes struggle for market share in Europe, the U.S., and Southeast Asia itself.

Hong Kong: The Chinese Money Laundry

During the 1960s, much of the region's opium was refined in Hong Kong itself; nowadays the colony serves largely as an entrepot and financial center for the area's narcotics traffic (Metcalfe and Wallen, 1988). Indeed, when U.S. officials recently analyzed the global flow of narcotics money, two key areas emerged: Panama for cocaine traffic and Hong Kong for heroin traffic (President's Commission, 1984). It is the immense profits emanating from the Golden Triangle drug trade that have strengthened the Chinese criminal organizations. These profits, washed in Hong Kong by willing bankers or secretly shipped abroad, are beginning to show up in San Francisco, Toronto, Vancouver, and New York City (Kaplan, Goldberg and Jue, 1986).

Hong Kong's banking industry acts as a conduit for drug money being moved from the U.S. to Hong Kong, and back again, for large-scale American importers and distributors, and for local Chinese drug traffickers who wish to diversify their assets by investing in North America (President's Commission, 1984). Just how much drug money is being laundered in Hong Kong no one knows, or can know, given the nature of Hong Kong's bank secrecy laws. But one indication came in August 1985, when U.S. Treasury Department officials fined California's Crocker National Bank a record US$2.5 million for violating the United States' Bank Secrecy Act by failing to report thousands of large cash transactions totaling US$3.89 billion during the previous five years.[2] Nearly all the money came from just six Hong Kong banks.[3]

While the Treasury Department took the position that there was a high probability that dirty money was being washed through Crocker National Bank, Crocker's general counsel, in press conferences, offered as excuse for failure to report the transactions, "mistakes in interpreting and implementing" regulations set forth in the Bank Secrecy Act. Indeed, some Crocker officials declared themselves as "outraged" at the very suggestion that the bank had deliberately laundered drug money (Kaplan, Goldberg and Jue, 1986; Mann, 1985).

Concerned about Hong Kong's possible role in this huge flow of cash, in 1984 the President's Commission on Organized Crime requested the Treasury Department to analyze all available U.S. data regarding financial transactions between the U.S. and Hong Kong. The results were striking. U.S. dollars — especially in small denominations — were accumulating in Hong Kong in phenomenal amounts. In 1982, one U.S. financial institution in Hong Kong handled approximately $700 million in U.S. currency, more than $1 billion in 1983, and more than $600 million in the first half of 1984. While about half of this currency is normally shipped to the United States, the balance, all in $100 bills, is shipped to other countries, principally Switzerland. Approximately 65% of the currency repatriated to the U.S. is in $100 bills. The remainder is in smaller-denomination bills, "a telltale sign of drug trafficking and money laundering," in the opinion of U.S. officials (President's Commission, 1984). Their suspicions were based on the fact that drug syndicates, whose profits frequently take the form of small bills, typically evade law enforcement by diverting cash to overseas banks (Karchmer, 1985). These institutions then deposit the funds in U.S. banks via wire transfers, often in accounts with assumed names. The overseas banks, left with piles of small bills, then ship them back to the U.S. in exchange for larger bills (Koepp, 1985). What makes these data particularly intriguing to some law enforcement authorities is that this consistent increase in U.S. currency repatriated from Hong Kong to the United States from 1982 to the first half of 1984 strikingly correlated with the steady increase in Southeast Asian heroin marketed in the U.S. from 1981 to 1983.

While there may be logical explanations to account for the annual repatriation of hundreds of millions of U.S. dollars in smaller-denomination bills from Hong Kong, it is the opinion of the President's Commission on Organized Crime that little credible evidence exists in support of such attempts. This volume of smaller-denomination bills exceeds the total volume of *all* currency transactions with any European country. In 1982, for example, total transfer of U.S. currency to and from Germany amounted to $12 million; from France, $8.8 million, while from Hong Kong — more than $100 million. Both Germany and France could reasonably be expected to have heavier tourist traffic and non-business contacts with the United States than does Hong Kong. Moreover, information available to the Treasury Department indicates that the flow of U.S. currency from the United States to Hong Kong is minimal when compared to the reverse flow of U.S. currency from Hong Kong.[4] Although the Treasury Department cites no evidence directly supporting a conclusion that the U.S. currency surplus in Hong Kong results from Southeast Asian drug trafficking, it is a logical and most compelling explanation for the inordinate surplus.

Where is all of this money going? Mostly, it would appear, to San Francisco. Treasury Department figures show that from 1980 through 1984, the amount of cash flowing to the States from Hong Kong jumped ten-fold, to more than US$1.7 billion. And almost 70% is believed to have gone directly into the San Francisco area. Moreover, after a decade of running cash deficits at the local Federal Reserve Bank, beginning in 1981 the San Francisco branch began to accumulate huge surpluses, almost tripling by 1985, so that at year's end San Francisco's Federal Reserve Bank had posted the second largest surplus of cash in the entire system — surpassed only by Miami (Kaplan, Goldberg, and Jue, 1986).

Hong Kong's favorable geographical position provides a bridge in the time-zone gap between North America and Europe. Together with its strong links to China and Southeast Asia and its excellent communications with the rest of the world, this has helped Hong Kong to develop as a significant international financial center. By the end of 1990, there were 166 licensed banks of which 80% were foreign. Foreign banks in Hong Kong represent nearly every major country in the world, and include 76 of the world's 100 largest banks. A substantial proportion of the banking transactions in Hong Kong are thus international in nature. Over 40% of the banking sector's aggregate assets and liabilities are external, spreading over more than 80 nations (Government Information Services, 1991).

In addition to standard banks, 46 restricted license banks and 191 quasi-banks, known as deposit-taking companies, were operating in Hong Kong at the end of 1990. These institutions, similar in some respects to American savings and loan firms and British building societies, have no checking accounts and have minimum asset requirements different from those of regular banks. They are permitted to make loans, pay higher rates of interest than banks and are given wire transfer authority. In addition to the banks and deposit-taking companies, there were also 151 representative offices of foreign banks, and 8415 licensed stock and commodity brokers and investment advisors operating in Hong Kong at the end of 1990.

The Hong Kong financial industry is further augmented by a vast cadre of attorneys specializing in international business and finance. This type of legal expertise is necessary for traffickers who desire to establish "shell" companies (that is, companies created specifically to handle large amounts of money moving through their various corporate bank accounts), to purchase property and vessels, and to move money. All this activity is cloaked in the anonymity provided by lawyers who administer trust accounts and business details (U.S. Department of Justice, 1983; Bartlett and Wallace, 1985).

In addition to the financial infrastructure described, still another banking system, sometimes referred to as the "underground" (Lee, Course, and Ng, 1988; Marsh, 1991) or "native banking system," exists outside the commercial banking sector and is estimated to be responsible for the transfer of significant amounts of drug money. This system, controlled almost exclusively by Chinese, is largely based on gold shops, trading companies and money changers, many of which are operated around the world by members of individual families. This system grew out of a combination of historical distrust for banks, political turmoil and communist takeovers in many countries where the Chinese resided and were constantly harassed. Out of necessity, the Chinese have developed a business style that, to Westerners, seems extremely secretive. However, bitter experience has taught these people well that the only reliable unit of business is the family.

The record-keeping procedures of the underground banking system are nearly non-existent. Coded messages, "chits" and simple telephone calls are used to transfer money from one country to another (Liu and Eads, 1985). The system inherently provides anonymity and security for the customer, converts gold or other items into currency and converts one currency into the currency of the customer's choice. When it is necessary to transfer money to

Southeast Asia from Europe or the United States, commercial bank facilities are utilized to augment the underground banking system.

With a vast majority of the Southeast Asian heroin trade controlled by Chinese criminal organizations, this underground banking system, coupled with a web of ethnic-based commercial contacts, creates a nearly impenetrable maze for law enforcement officials to work their way through. One Hong Kong police official has stated that he once seized a piece of paper with the picture of an elephant on it that represented the collection receipt for $3 million at a Hong Kong gold shop. Wire taps placed on some of the major gold shops and trading companies by both Thai and Hong Kong police have documented large transfers of suspected drug money. In Hong Kong however, these wire transfers are used only to locate and identify drug shipments. Information concerning currency movement is discarded (U.S. Department of Justice, 1983).

Unlike the United States, Hong Kong has neither central bank nor currency exchange controls, thus virtually eliminating the possibility of tracing funds entering or leaving Hong Kong.[5] Moreover, Hong Kong law firmly protects the colony's status as a financial secrecy jurisdiction (hereafter referred to as a FSJ). All FSJs seek, at a minimum, to preserve their status as secure havens for the billions of dollars which are not derived from drug trafficking and other criminal activities (Nadelmann, 1986). However, in moving money to an offshore FSJ, investors may run the risk of landing in a jurisdiction where there is too little government control and not enough policing of potential fraud. Hong Kong, however, satisfies the requirement for secrecy within a fairly well-regulated banking system, especially if the customer invests only with the colony's major financial institutions. Hong Kong's bank secrecy law bars insight by national and foreign authorities alike. The law declares certain records held by financial institutions, generally describing ownership or control of accounts, to be confidential. Disclosure of data contained in such records may create civil or criminal liability. Further enhancing Hong Kong's status as a FSJ is the presence of so-called "blocking statutes," which effectively prevent the disclosure, copying, inspection or removal of documents located in the host country in compliance with orders by foreign authorities. Hong Kong's blocking statute prohibits local residents from disclosing certain information or records to non-residents and from complying with orders of foreign authorities to produce such information or records.[6]

Drug traffickers are the world's biggest consumers of money-laundering services. Just as good businessmen everywhere, they prefer to diversify their assets and invest in legitimate businesses. Consequently they need to conceal the connection between their globe-trotting funds and the crimes that earned them. Once in an anonymous bank account in a FSJ, however, cash can be safely invested for the customer's benefit. To throw law enforcement officials off the "paper trail," money can be easily switched from one account, or bank, to another — preferably with conversions into and out of cash along the way. In addition to the secrecy provided by bank accounts, sophisticated money launderers often own international trading companies whose payments move in uncheckable directions. For example, how can police question how much a Hong Kong trading company paid for Thai cement, and how much it then charged the builders of a Malaysian hotel for the material? The Hong Kong company can simply name a figure and deposit it in a bank — and explain how it came by the money (Finance, 1988).

American law enforcement agents are at a severe disadvantage when they try to collect information and evidence of American crimes from abroad. Perhaps the greatest handicap in this area is the legal barrier that financial secrecy laws erect between law enforcement agents and financial records in FSJs such as Hong Kong. While Hong Kong law enforcement officials can occasionally gain access to banking records by proving to a court that their need for the information is reasonable, the local banking law does not permit law enforcement "fishing expeditions" regarding the criminal use of bank accounts. American bankers and U.S. Consulate officials in Hong Kong observe that while the guarantees of secrecy in Hong Kong might not be perfect, they are nevertheless, by American standards, extremely rigid.

Obviously, a banking industry the size of Hong Kong's deals in tremendous sums of money from every conceivable kind of commerce. Some local bankers, however, are rather sensitive to accusations of possible drug links to their industry. While they readily agree that their organizations routinely deposit large sums of U.S. currency with West Coast banks, they claim the funds come largely from daily foreign-exchange transactions with residents of the Philippines, Taiwan, Singapore, Thailand, and other countries in the region (Liu and Eads, 1985). There is considerably less agreement on what percentage of the currency[7] flowing through the system is generated from the drug trade. As one Hong Kong-based British banker explained, the United Kingdom, like Hong Kong, has less stringent currency controls than does the United States. "So why don't we say money is being laundered in the U.K.?," he asked defiantly.[8] However, an American banker, also based in Hong Kong, has remarked: "For banking, Hong Kong is a wild and woolly place. Banking here is very, very competitive. It's tough. There are banks here that are apparently willing to play fast and loose with credit, and even with the law" (Mann, 1985). In such a competitive market, banks and brokerage companies often compete, not always unwittingly, for highly questionable business. Under such conditions, even banks with high professional standards are reasonably comfortable in the stance that such large cash deposits are simply "black" (that is, untaxed or from the "underground economy") rather than "dirty."

For many Hong Kong government officials, money laundering is one of those problems that fall into the "too-difficult-to-handle" category. Recently, and only under intense pressure from foreign governments, Hong Kong has begun to face the possibility that large-scale money laundering may indeed be occurring in the colony. With a view to deciding what actions to take, Hong Kong officials have held a number of informal meetings with U.S. officials at which the Americans have expressed their concerns. In late 1987, Hong Kong's Acting Commissioner for Narcotics told reporters: "The U.S. is very keen and concerned about this problem and has been urging us to implement legislation as soon as possible. The U.S. Consul General has held meetings with us at a policy-making level. We have been trying to get across the message that Hong Kong is trying to do something" (Dear, 1987). Despite such assurances, additional remarks made by the Acting Commissioner during that interview indicate attitudes — denial, naivete, complacency, and outright disingenuousness — which some government critics claim have stalled meaningful efforts to come to grips with the problem of money laundering. In short, the basic problem appears to be a widespread lack of political will to deal effectively with this and other various manifestations of white-collar crime in Hong Kong (Mulcahy, 1987).

While a number of senior Hong Kong government officials reject allegations of large-scale money laundering in the colony, they are at odds with the local police. One officer cites examples of people taking cash out of the U.S. in suitcases, legally laundering it in Hong Kong and then re-investing it in legitimate businesses in the U.S. Over and over, one hears local police exports toll similar stories. A key barrier to progress in stemming the international flow of drug money, apparently, is the fear on the part of some government and banking officials that banking business could be lost to neighbors if the policy of bank secrecy was undermined. This concern was voiced during a recent workshop on economic crime held in Hong Kong under the auspices of the Commonwealth Secretariat and Crown Agents (Mulcahy, 1987).

Sophisticated criminals know that putting evidence abroad makes it more difficult for U.S. officials to discover it. Due to the fact that U.S. laws on money laundering have recently been sharpened and strengthened, the United States is becoming a very unaccommodating place to store or launder illegal cash (see Banking, 1988). Traffickers, however, have learned to direct an entire global network of illegal operations by moving with anonymous ease through the international community (Grilli, 1987).

Reflecting the concern shown by a number of countries, Hong Kong police are beginning to shift their focus from chasing criminals to chasing criminal funds. But at this point, the police are not getting much help from the bankers themselves who realize that the colony's reputation as the "Switzerland of Asia" is a key reason for its impressive growth as a banking center. As the managing director of a prominent bank put it: "It's not our business to inquire into our client's morals" (Liu and Eads, 1985). This banker's candid remark seems to be a clear rebuff of the government's desire to consult with the banking industry on how money is laundered in Hong Kong.

Political Instability, Capital Flight, and Hot Money

To this point I have tried to present the case for Hong Kong as one of the world's leading money laundering centers. That case rests, ultimately, on the credibility and persuasiveness of a number of data sources: historical records; U.S. government statistics; and interviews with informed bankers, journalists, government officials, academics, and foreign diplomats in Hong Kong. The taken-for-granted status of money laundering in Hong Kong would seem to mark any attempt to make a case against Hong Kong as one of the world's leading money laundering centers as doomed to failure. However, a number of Hong Kong's bankers and government officials have tried to make just such a case. What are their arguments and can they stand the test of close scrutiny?

In late 1985, when the American Assistant Secretary of the Treasury announced the US$2.5 million fine against California's Crocker National Bank for failure to comply with the United States' Bank Secrecy Act, he strongly suggested that the money may have resulted from criminal activity. By failing to report the cash transactions, he stated, Crocker had "deprived Treasury of potentially important law-enforcement leads that could have been useful in drug, tax, money laundering, and other investigations." His remarks not only angered Crocker Bank executives, but also banking and government officials in Hong Kong who complained bitterly that there is "no good reason to assume" that the large dollar deposits were necessarily the result of drug trafficking or any other illicit activity. In their view, there are many other factors, mostly related to the politics and finance of East Asia, that could legitimately account for the cash shipments (Mann, 1985).

Hong Kong banking officials argued that the cash was flown to San Francisco simply to take advantage of airline schedules, permitting the money to be deposited in a timely way so that interest could begin to accrue in Crocker Bank on the same day it left Hong Kong. In 1985, a daily Pan American flight leaving Hong Kong at 1:30 p.m. arrived in San Francisco (having crossed the International Date Line) at 10:15 a.m. the same day. No flight to New York City offered the same banking benefit. While one must concede the reasonableness of this argument, the question still remains: How did Hong Kong banks happen to have all those dollar bills? As we have already learned, because of the bank secrecy law and the prevailing Hong Kong ethos of not asking too many questions, no one can say for sure. While the U.S. Treasury Department and the President's Commission on Organized Crime have made known their brooding suspicions, many Hong Kong bankers, government officials, and foreign diplomats argue that such suspicions of illicit activities overlook what was happening in Hong Kong and the rest of East Asia in the first half of the 1980s. In this alternative reading of events, the period mentioned by the President's Commission, from 1982 to 1984, was the peak time for capital flight from Hong Kong. Negotiations were then underway between China and Britain over the future of the colony. These negotiations coincided perfectly with the years of capital flight and ended in 1984 with the signing of the Sino-British Joint Declaration in which it was agreed that Hong Kong would be transferred to the People's Republic of China in 1997.

Moreover, in the early years of this period the value of the Hong Kong dollar fell precipitously and there was a rush to convert savings and assets to U.S. dollars.[9] Nervous businessmen were selling goods, even their factories, and insisting on receiving cash in U.S. currency. With the Hong Kong dollar declining in value, Hong Kong shops began quoting prices in U.S. dollars, and Hong Kong banks began competing for deposits by advertising U.S. dollar accounts. In early 1982, U.S. dollar accounts made up only 17% of all bank deposits in Hong Kong. By 1984 the figure was nearly 50%. To these events must be added the fact that Hong Kong has traditionally carried out much more business in cash than is done in the United States.

Finally, Hong Kong officials argue that the U.S. dollar outflows are also a natural consequence of the fact that Hong Kong is the main financial center for other countries in the region. Many citizens of these countries use Hong Kong as a remitting center for all sorts of transactions, both business and personal. This additional business contributes enormously to Hong Kong's indigenous U.S. dollar volume. According to this scenario, when rich businessmen in the Philippines or Taiwan want to remove funds for investment in the United States or to send to relatives there, they do so through Hong Kong. And when overseas Chinese entrepreneurs in Malaysia or Indonesia become fearful of possible discrimination against them, they may move their money to Hong Kong. Since all these other countries have exchange controls, a suitcase full of U.S. dollars is a convenient, if cumbersome, way of transporting money. The colony's defenders argue that these factors contributed to the big increase in U.S. currency within Hong Kong's banks in the early 1980s (Mann, 1985).

Together, these arguments make a strong case for the "exceptional" quality of Hong Kong's banking system. Yet, notwithstanding the validity of the arguments, one would have to be a Polyanna indeed to deny the existence of money laundering in Hong Kong. While it is true that one must look at Hong Kong with an Asian perspective, and that comparisons between, say, the Cayman Islands and Hong Kong are perhaps unjustified, Hong Kong is undeniably the center of "hot money" for the region. For Hong Kong officials to strike a see-no-evil posture does their credibility no good.

After years of denying that money laundering was occurring in the colony, Hong Kong's government has finally begun to acknowledge the obvious. In 1989, police estimated that HK$6 million in drug money was being laundered in Hong Kong each day (Hewett, 1990). That same year, a special unit, the Narcotics Bureau's Financial Investigations Group, was established to enforce a significant piece of new legislation, the Drug Trafficking (Recovery of Proceeds) Ordinance 1989.[10] As of April 1990, HK$375 million of alleged drug money had been seized by the Narcotics Bureau pending the trial of persons charged with trafficking offenses. Under the new legislation, assets may be confiscated by the courts following a criminal conviction and a civil proceeding in which the government has won the right of confiscation.

Bank secrecy is not so strict now.[11] The law requires financial institutions under restraining orders to co-operate with the authorities. Inaction can lead an institution to be held in contempt of court, and individuals involved may face criminal charges. As a result, banks and other financial institutions have appointed "compliance officers" whose job it is to detect and report suspected drug proceeds. Some trust companies now demand bank and character references of new clients, along with financial histories (Hewett, 1990). Under the ordinance, much of the burden of enforcement has been passed on to the banks since they are now liable themselves if they can be shown to have handled drug money, even if unwittingly.

Yet, in the absence of firm evidence, no one is now able to say with complete certainty what percentage of Hong Kong's banking business is attributable to money laundering. Hong Kong's total lack of controls on the movement of currency, its guarantees of very tight secrecy for depositors, and a colony-wide banking ethos that puts the bottom line near the top, allow government and banking officials to posture and protest as they will. Which, in the end, is perhaps precisely the way they and thousands of Hong Kong's bank customers hope the situation will remain.

Notes

1. Money laundering "is the process by which one conceals the existence, illegal source, or illegal application of income, and then disguises that income to make it appear legitimate" (President's Commission, 1984). The

term is derived from the argot, or specialized vocabulary, of criminals who refer to "dirty" or "black" cash being "washed" so it can be used openly.

2. Crocker National Bank was not the only institution to be fined under the Bank Secrecy Act. In February of the same year, the U.S government indicted the First National Bank of Boston for its failure to report cash shipments to nine foreign banks, primarily three in Switzerland, involving more than $1.2 billion. Between 1981 and 1985, First National received $529 million, mainly in small bills (weight: at least 20 tons), and sent out $690 million in bills generally of $100 or more. First National pleaded guilty and was fined $500 000. Within a month of this conviction, the Shawmut Bank of Boston disclosed that it had engaged in 1800 separate transactions with seven foreign banks that should have been reported to the Comptroller of the Currency under section 5316 of the Bank Secrecy Act. Other banks that made similar disclosures in this period include Manufacturer's Hanover Trust, Irving Trust, Chemical Bank, Bank of New York and First National Bank of Chicago. In early 1986, the Bank of America was fined a record $4.75 million for failing to report more than 17 000 large cash transactions (Koepp, 1985).

3. The six Hong Kong banks named by the Department of the Treasury as involved in the Crocker National Bank transaction were the Wing Hang Bank, Wing Lung Bank, Hang Seng Bank, Hong Kong Industrial and Commercial Bank, Hang Lung Bank, and the Overseas Trust Bank.

Interestingly, both the Hang Lung Bank and Overseas Trust Bank collapsed between late 1983 and the summer of 1984. In both cases, bank executives were charged with misappropriation of funds. Of the two banks, the failure of the Overseas Trust Bank was the more spectacular as it involved the fourth-largest locally incorporated bank in Hong Kong, with 120 000 depositors and 44 branches.

On the very night of the day government officials declared the Overseas Trust Bank insolvent and closed it, Patrick Chang Chen Tsong, the bank's chief executive officer and son of the bank's founder, was arrested at Hong Kong's Kai Tak Airport as he was about to abscond with US$154 000 in cash and US$1.54 million in securities hidden in his briefcase. The cost to Hong Kong's tax payers of the government's bail-out of the bank is estimated at more than US$250 million.

Curiously, when asked by American reporters whether there may have been a connection between the cash transactions with Crocker National Bank and events leading up to the Overseas Trust Bank's insolvency, a Hong Kong and Shanghai Banking Corporation official who was then serving as managing director of the government-run bank, replied: "I don't know, myself. I haven't made any inquires." He continued: "As far as we're concerned, under the new management we buy and sell foreign currency notes at OTB. There is a lot of business in U.S. dollars. We buy more U.S. dollars than we sell and every so often we ship the excess dollars to the United States. There's nothing illegal about it as far as Hong Kong banks are concerned. It's unfortunate that Crocker didn't report it" (Mann, 1985).

4. While this is literally true, it is not to be taken as proof that U.S. dollars are not entering Hong Kong from the United States. On the one hand, cash is easily smuggled out of the U.S. ("The majority of narcotics money is flown out. It's that simple.") And, at a higher level of sophistication, there is the telegrahic or wire transfer, which is responsible for exporting huge volumes of money each day. American bank officers, as a discretionary service to their customers, will agree to enter on their records false foreign account number destinations. They may also assist in fraudulent identification of source orders by not recording the actual source, and, by "being away from their desk," arrange that another officer who has not received the wire transfer order signs it as received. This device circumvents follow-up on "errors" in address recording. Such errors are, in any event, not at all uncommon in wire transfer departments (Committee on Governmental Affairs, 1983).

5. It is perfectly legal to enter Hong Kong with a suitcase stuffed with cash. There are no restrictions whatsoever on the import, export, purchase, or sale of foreign currency. Nor are there any currency declaration forms to be filled out upon entry.

6. A number of countries other than those usually identified as tax or secrecy havens have comprehensive blocking statutes to guard their sovereignty from the extraterritorial reach of foreign authorities. These include the United Kingdom, France, South Africa, Germany, Australia, New Zealand, Norway and Canada.

7. The vast majority of all funds handled by the Hong Kong banks is in U.S. dollars, followed (a distant second) by Japanese yen, British pounds and German marks (U.S. Department of Justice, 1983).

8. Many experts consider the Channel Islands and the Isle of Man to be important FSJs.

9. In 1983, in the wake of all this uncertainty, the Hong Kong dollar was pegged at 7.80 to the U.S. dollar. However, the peg, which is still in force as of April 1992, is under a new threat, this time precipitated by a weakened U.S. currency.

10. While the Hong Kong government may have wished to jump on this particular bandwagon, they almost certainly were also dragged onto it. There have been a number of international instruments in relation to drug smuggling and money laundering, including the *United Nations Convention Against Illicit Traffic in Narcotic Drugs and Psychotropic Substances (1988)*, to which the U.K. is a signatory. In addition, a number of other international groups have discussed such problems, including the "Trevi Group," membership of which comprises the ministers of justice of various European countries, including the U.K. Home Secretary. In addition, a Financial Action Task Force was set up in 1989 to address the problem, under the auspices of the European Commission. Again, the the U.K. is a member. In short, the Hong Kong government must have been under some pressure from the U.K. to come into line with the thinking of international governmental groups on this issue.

11. For an analysis of legal changes pertaining to bank secrecy in the U.K. itself, see Levi, 1991.

References

Banking. 1988. "A Drug Bust at the Laundry." October 28, 1988. *Asiaweek* 14: 60-61.

Bartlett, Sarah and G. David Wallace. 1985. "Money Laundering: Who's Involved, How it Works, and Where it's Spreading." March 18, 1985. *Business Week* 214: 74-80.

Block, Alan A. and William J. Chambliss. 1981. *Organizing Crime*. New York: Elsevier.

Camens, Jane. 1988. "Hong Kong at center of drug empire." Hong Kong: *Hong Kong Standard* (April 1)

Committee on Governmental Affairs. 1983. *Crime and Secrecy: The Use of Offshore Banks and Companies*. Washington, D.C.: U.S. Government Printing Office.

Crisswell, Colin and Mike Watson. 1982. *The Royal Hong Kong Police Force (1841-1945)*. Hong Kong: Macmillan.

Crowell, Todd and Tsang Shuk Wa. 1988. "Unmasking the Triads." November 11, 1988. *Asiaweek* 14: 52-57.

Dear, Justin. 1987. "Move to hit traffickers where it really hurts." Hong Kong: *Hong Kong Standard* (October 25).

————. 1988. "Hong Kong king nabbed after four year chase." Hong Kong: *Hong Kong Standard* (March 16).

Dubro, Alec and David E. Kaplan 1986. *Yakuza*. New York: Addison-Wesley.

Finance. 1988. "Cleaning up dirty laundering." August 20, 1988. *The Economist* 308: 65-66.

Freemantle, Brian. 1985. *The Fix*. London: Michael Joseph.

Government Information Services. 1991. *Hong Kong 1991*. Hong Kong: Hong Kong Government Printer.

Grilli, Andrea M. 1987. "Preventing Billions From Being Washed Offshore: A Growing Approach to Stopping International Drug Trafficking." *Syracuse Journal of International Law and Commerce* 14: 65-88.

Hewett, Gareth. 1990. "Police freeze $375m alleged drug money." Hong Kong: *South China Morning Post* (April 8).

Kaplan, David E., Donald Goldberg and Linda Jue. 1986. "Enter the Dragon." December. *San Francisco Focus*: 68-79.

Karchmer, Clifford L.1985. "Money laundering and the organized underworld." In Herbert E. Alexander and Gerald E. Caiden (eds.), *The Politics and Economics of Organized Crime*. Lexington, MA: Lexington Books.

Kerr, Peter. 1988. "Chinese muscle in on the mafia and heroin dealers." Hong Kong: *Hong Kong Standard* (January 5).

Koepp, Stephen. 1985. "Dirty cash and tarnished vaults." February 25, 1985. *Time* 125: 65.

Lee, Jacqueline, Lindy Course and Elizabeth Ng. 1988. "Family on drug charges face U.S. extradition." Hong Kong: *South China Morning Post* (July 27).

Levi, Michael. 1991. "Regulating Money Laundering: The Death of Bank Secrecy in the U.K." *The British Journal of Criminology* 31:109-125.

Liu, Melinda and Brian Eads. 1985. "Hong Kong's funny money." September 23, 1985. *Newsweek* 106: 52.

Mann, Jim. 1985. "U.S. wary of Hong Kong's bank secrecy." Los Angeles: *Los Angeles Times* (September 15).

Marsh, Jon. 1991. "HK on the mainline." Hong Kong: *South China Morning Post* (March 24).

McCoy, Alfred W. 1972. *The Politics of Heroin in Southeast Asia*. New York: Harper and Row.

Metcalfe, Tim and David Wallen. 1988. "World drug ring arrests reveal Hong Kong as key staging post." Hong Kong: *South China Morning Post* (July 27)

Mulcahy, John. 1987. "The Chinese Laundry." August 20, 1987. *Far Eastern Economic Review* 137: 54.

Nadelmann, Ethan A. 1986. *Unlaundering Dirty Money Abroad: U.S. Foreign Policy and Financial Secrecy Jurisdictions*. Cambridge, MA: Center for International Affairs.

President's Commission on Organized Crime. 1984. *The Cash Connection: Organized Crime, Financial Institutions, and Money Laundering*. Washington, D.C.: U.S. Government Printing Office.

Seagrave, Sterling. 1985. *The Soong Dynasty*. New York: Harper and Row.

U.S. Department of Justice. 1983. *Operation Cashflow: The Movement and Impact of International Drug Money*. Washington, D.C.: U.S. Government Printing Office.

6

The Yakuza and Amphetamine Abuse in Japan

Masayuki Tamura

Organized crime in Japan is dominated by several large, nationwide syndicates collectively referred to as the Yakuza. The Yakuza have a long and colorful history and their own peculiar subculture. They are involved in a number of illicit activities, but their most lucrative one derives from their control of the drug trade. Current drug problems in Japan include glue sniffing among juveniles and the intravenous injection of stimulants (methamphetamines and amphetamines) among the adult population. In connection with these two problems, the Yakuza almost completely monopolize the illegal distribution and sale of stimulants.

The Organization of the Yakuza

The Yakuza have approximately 90 000 members in 3200 local groups, organized into several nationwide syndicates. The three largest national syndicates are Yamaguchi-gumi, Inagawa-kai and Sumiyoshi-rengo. In all, 36% of the individual members and 40% of the groups fall within the sphere of influence of those three large organizations (National Police Agency, 1988a).

The activities of the Yakuza have become a heavy burden to the Japanese criminal justice system. Yakuza members account for 30% of the murders, 16% of the robberies, 22% of the serious assaults and 15% of the reported rapes (Ministry of Justice, 1988). Of Japan's total prison population, Yakuza members comprise approximately 30%, and these men are the main source of trouble for prison officials. Their activities, however, are changing from the commission of violent offenses to the provision of illegal services such as gambling, drugs, prostitution, and the control of legitimate businesses such as construction companies, restaurants, bars, night clubs, and finance companies.

In order to seek lucrative opportunities in smuggling drugs, guns, and prostitutes, the Yakuza have extended their operations into other Asian countries: Korea, Hong Kong, Taiwan and the Philippines; as well as into Hawaii, Guam, and the mainland of the United States.

Organized criminal gangs in Japan are divided into three types according to their origin: Bakuto, Tekiya, and others. The word Yakuza originally meant "Bakuto," but in common parlance today it is used as a collective term for all organized criminal gangs that adopt traditional methods for organizing their members. The origin of Bakuto and Tekiya can be traced back to the middle of the Tokugawa Period (1603-1867). Bakuto was an organization of gamblers, labor contractors, and hoodlums, whose main activity was gambling. Tekiya, on the other hand, was an organization of peddlers of medicines and small commodities who traveled from town to town. Although those traditional activities are preserved in both groups even now, modern gangs are becoming similar to each other with respect to both legal and illegal activities.

The most distinctive feature of Yakuza subculture is the loyalty and voluntary subordination of ordinary members to the gang's leadership. The cohesiveness of the group and the strength of the line of command are derived from their being organized on quasi-familial lines which, not coincidentally, also happen to be characteristic of Japanese society. For example, the leader and his subordinates exchange a *sake* cup to affirm a father-son relationship in the ritual for admission to the group or "family."

A Brief History of Drug Use in Japan

Until World War II Japan did not face a serious drug problem. Illegal drug activity in Japan has developed mainly in the postwar era and can be divided into three distinctive periods.

The first, lasting from 1945 to 1956, was characterized by an explosive growth in the use of stimulant drugs. By 1954 it was estimated there were 550 000 active stimulant drug users (Tatetsu, Goto and Fujiwara, 1956). Increased law enforcement efforts, followed by the enactment of the Stimulant Control Law of 1951 (amendmented in 1954 and 1956), is credited with largely terminating that epidemic. The number of violations of the Stimulant Control Law declined from 55 000 in the peak year of 1954 to a mere 271 in 1958.

The second period, from 1957 to 1969, was a quiet one compared to the stimulant drug problem, with approximately 500 arrests yearly. However, some stimulant users were said to be turning to narcotics or other depressants in substitution for stimulants, and some areas experienced isolated outbreaks of narcotic and sedative abuse. The peak in narcotic offenses (heroin) occurred in 1962 when 2349 people were arrested for violation of the Narcotics Control Law. A sleeping pill craze among street youth in Tokyo in 1960 was seen as the forerunner of a period of drug abuse among juveniles. In 1967, a glue-sniffing epidemic started, and some 40 000 juveniles were put under protective custody for sniffing glue and paint thinner. Arrests for this offense have continued at roughly that number ever since.

The third period started in 1970 when the number of people arrested for stimulant drug abuse started to increase rapidly. The number of arrests doubled each year until 1974 when stronger measures were introduced through a 1973 amendment to the Stimulant Control Law. The subsequent decline in stimulant drug abuse was widely attributed to the introduction of harsher criminal sanctions. However, the effect, if one existed, lasted only a year. There were over 10 000 arrests in 1976 and 20 000 in 1981, and the number has remained at that level (Table 1).

The statistics for 1987 show that the Japanese police arrested 20 643 persons for violation of the Stimulant Control Law and confiscated 620 kg of stimulants, the highest record for confiscation in Japanese history. It is noteworthy that 45% of those persons arrested were Yakuza, and it is the Yakuza that control the stimulant distribution system in Japan today. In order to fully understand the current drug epidemic, we must look at the activities of the Yakuza organizations.

Table 1 Number of Arrestees for Drug Control Law Violations, 1954–90.

Year	Stimulant violations	Narcotics violations	Cannabis violations
1954	55 664	–	–
1955	32 140	–	–
1956	5 047	1 103	15
1957	781	1 188	22
1958	271	1 667	6
1959	372	1 525	29
1960	476	2 081	11
1961	477	1 954	34
1962	546	2 349	55
1963	971	2 288	146
1964	860	847	185
1965	735	859	201
1966	694	692	176
1967	675	476	290
1968	775	227	338
1969	704	130	315
1970	1 682	110	487
1971	2 634	119	518
1972	4 709	204	518
1973	8 301	325	617
1974	5 919	276	588
1975	8 218	150	733
1976	10 678	84	735
1977	14 447	98	892
1978	17 740	61	1 070
1979	18 297	49	1 041
1980	19 921	113	1 173
1981	22 024	59	1 122
1982	23 365	64	1 083
1983	23 301	66	1 035
1984	24 022	108	1 230
1985	22 980	115	1 099
1086	21 052	85	1 171
1987	20 643	82	1 276
1988	20 399	105	1 464
1989	16 613	205	1 344
1990	15 038	186	1 512

(National Police Agency, 1991)

The Current Epidemic and the Yakuza

The second stimulant epidemic started around 1970. At that time, the Yakuza had come to dominate the supply of stimulants, marking a major change from the earlier stimulant epidemic (1945-56). In the early 1970s, many gang leaders and members, imprisoned earlier by the "first operation on top ranks" conducted by the police in the 1960s, were released from prison and started to look for lucrative activities that could serve as a basis for reorganizing their gangs. This allegedly led to the Yakuza's re-entry into the stimulant business. Some observers have reported that during the construction of the Osaka Expo World Fair, construction workers were introduced to stimulants by these gangs and then returned to their home districts with stimulant drug dependencies. In any event, the new epidemic appears to have started in the Osaka area and gradually spread to Tokyo and northern Japan as additional crime syndicates, such as Yamaguchi-gumi, spread their organizations throughout Japan.

There are four reasons why the Yakuza came to dominate the business of trafficking in stimulants. First, the gang organization permitted an easy involvement in illicit and covert activities that required a considerable degree of co-ordination. Second, there were no equally lucrative sources of income for the Yakuza at that time. Third, profits of this activity provided resources to expand the Yakuza's sphere of influence over local gangs. Fourth, Yakuza members themselves were habitual users of stimulants. They believe strongly in concepts such as physical prowess, masculinity, aggressiveness, hedonism, and fatalism. Stimulants relieve, if only temporarily, fatigue and boredom, lift sagging spirits and reinforce confidence and bravery. Such effects are completely consistent with the masculine image that Japanese gangsters have of themselves (Fukushima 1977).

Today, virtually all stimulants are illegally imported from Taiwan, Korea, the Philippines, and other Asian countries with which the Yakuza have connections. The Yakuza almost exclusively deal in stimulants in spite of the ready availability of heroin in Southeast Asia.

Why do the Japanese use these particular stimulants rather than the narcotics or hallucinogens popular in many Western countries? We can only speculate, but the following explanations are noteworthy (Tamura, 1982):

First, in terms of demand, gang members traditionally do not like to use narcotics or hallucinogens, and they believe that demand for these drugs would be weak. Therefore, they are reluctant to deal in drugs other than stimulants. Second, narcotics have been viewed historically as dangerous drugs leading to a loss of nationhood, as occurred in China during the Opium Wars. On the other hand, stimulants are viewed as less dangerous, even with the experience of the first epidemic. Third, it has been speculated that a sense of nationalism on the part of criminal gangs may also have influenced the decision to select stimulants rather than the narcotics associated with some of Japan's Asian neighbors. Fourth, the choice of stimulants may be well suited to a people seen as having workaholic tendencies. Japanese culture places a strong value on showing diligence, while spurning idleness or even extended periods of relaxation. Finally, while narcotics and hallucinogenic drugs can be viewed as allowing the user to dream, stimulant drugs are thought to allow the realization of dreams. If one's dream is to become a superman and achieve a position of superiority over others, narcotics and hallucinogens are inadequate and ill-suited. Stimulants, on the other hand, allow a person to view himself as superhuman and capable of achieving fantastic feats of physical and sexual potency.

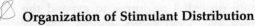

Organization of Stimulant Distribution

In the first epidemic, stimulants originally came from military stocks, through illegal channels from pharmaceutical companies and from underground factories in Japan. The source of supply changed, however, as laws regulating the production and flow of stimulants were enacted. Today it is thought to be foolhardy to make stimulants in domestic underground factories, as the flow of raw materials for stimulants is also strictly controlled by law, and the clandestine laboratories have a good chance of being discovered and raided by the police. In addition, domestically produced stimulants are considerably more expensive than imported stimulants. Yakuza groups, therefore, depend on connections with other Asian countries for supplies. As the yen appreciated against the U.S. dollar in the late 1980s, the import price of stimulants decreased from around 3000 yen per gram in late 1970 to less than 2000 yen.

Based on the confiscation data available, it was estimated that in 1980, 79% of stimulants in Japan came from Korea and 21% from Taiwan (National Police Agency, 1981). But the sources of supply changed as the so-called "social purification activities" were stengthened in Korea to eliminate criminals and hoodlums in preparation for the 1988 Seoul Olympic Games. By 1987 it was estimated that 78% of stimulants came from Taiwan and only 11% from Korea (National Police Agency, 1988b). This change suggests that effective drug control can only be achieved through international co-operation.

The stimulant distribution system is monopolized by Yakuza groups. However, there were some cases where non-Yakuza businessmen tried to avoid bankruptcy by illicitly importing stimulants. In one case a businessman could not find a way to sell the drugs in Japan and was finally defrauded by Yakuza members to whom he had turned to help sell his drugs. Amateurs who do not have connections with the Yakuza and who are not able to protect themselves from the considerable risks and violence inherent in the illegal drug business are almost never successful in the drug dealing business.

Stimulants flow from the top of the distribution system (importer and wholesaler) through several mid-level dealers to street-level dealers before reaching the customer. A large majority of the dealers are gang members or persons who have relations with local gangs. Only at the bottom level are there dealers who do not have some form of gang affiliation.

Interview With a Wholesale Dealer

This section reports information derived from interviews conducted by the author with arrested drug dealers in Osaka area police stations in November 1982. The interviews describe how the dealers conducted their activities and made profits from drug dealing (Tamura 1983).

Mr. I, a 49 year-old member of the Hiroshima-based Yakuza K organization, is a chief of the Osaka branch office. Mr. I spoke very politely and looked very much like a kind uncle, but in his youth he had been a short-tempered and violent man and had served three prison terms. He had used stimulants in the first epidemic, but not the second.

Three years ago he was asked to assist the wholesale drug business of Mr. A of the M family in Osaka. Mr. I had known Mr. A for ten years because the K family and the M family were friendly with one another and a quasi-brotherhood had been established between the bosses of the two families. Mr. A was believed to be importing stimulants concealed in furniture from Korea. Although Mr. I did not know how much Mr. A imported, he did know that Mr. A had built a luxurious house in the suburbs and that he owned a nightclub in a fashionable district of downtown Osaka. Mr. I assumed, therefore, that Mr. A was dealing in large amounts of stimulants.

At Mr. A's request, Mr. I started distributing drugs in and around the Osaka area. One year later he became an independent wholesaler, buying his supplies from Mr. A and selling to local dealers. Mr. I had several distribution routes with local gangs with which the K family had friendly relations. The price paid to Mr. A was 500 000 to 550 000 yen per 100 grams, and the price at which Mr. I sold to his local dealers was 700 000 to 750 000 yen.

Mr. I brought in drugs by himself when sales occurred in the Osaka vicinity, and he was paid in cash so that there is no evidence of the transactions. If the place of sale was far from Osaka and involved a trusted customer, he would send drugs concealed in gift parcels using women's names as sender and recipient to avoid attracting the attention of law enforcement agencies. He also used bank accounts for transactions.

A 100-gram transaction netted Mr. I, on average, 150 000 yen profit, but some dealings involved the non-profit distribution of drugs to subordinate local gangs within his family for their financial support. He reported it took 10 kg, or 100 dealings of 100 g, to earn 10 million yen. Thus, the wholesale business was only moderately profitable. The largest profits went to the importers and street dealers. Although importers require a large amount of capital, they can quickly amass large profits because the size of a deal at any one time might be very large (1 kg or more). Street dealers, on the other hand, need not have capital: they simply sell drugs to as many customers as possible.

Because his customers were gang members who were affiliated with his family or with groups friendly with his family, Mr. I had not anticipated discovery and arrest as a dealer. It is strictly forbidden for Yakuza members to disclose inside matters of the family to outsiders, especially to the police. However, his name had nonetheless managed to become known through one of the distribution routes in which he had placed his trust.

Interview With a Middle-Level Dealer

Thirty-nine year old Mr. N was a member of the Osaka-based O family. He had been arrested eight previous times, including three times for violating the Stimulant Control Law, and he had been released from his third imprisonment just 18 months before the interview. With a blunt, tough face and a deep scar from forehead to cheek, he appeared to be a typically dauntless Yakuza member. Mr. N began using stimulants in 1972 when he was a long-distance truck driver, resorting to them twice daily to help him remain awake at night. He entered the drug trade as a dealer upon his first release from prison.

Mr. N revealed he had several sources from which to buy stimulants, but that his main supply route was the O organization. He noted that many supply routes were needed in the business in order to buy high quality drugs at a favorable price, and for securing supply in case of a drug shortage. Additionally, having numerous sources was useful in case of problems with the police. When he was arrested and interrogated by the police, he could disclose a source of supply to which he felt no obligation and could conceal other sources. If he disclosed the name of a member of his organization as a source of supply, naturally he could not expect continued assistance from the organization. Moreover, he would be subject to retaliation from the organization's members even in prison, as well as after his release.

Mr. N believed that the stimulants flowed from an importer through a wholesaler to the boss of O organization, and then on to him, but he did not know exactly at what level of the distribution system he stood. Even though the stimulants supplied from O organization were known for their quality, sometimes he received adulterated drugs because someone at a higher level had added some substance in order to make more profit.

Typically, Mr. N would purchase 10 g of stimulants for 60 000 yen and divide this into smaller, 0.4 g packages to be sold for around 10 000 yen each. In a month, he normally sold 100 g of stimulants, which totaled 2 million yen. The total buying-in price was 600 000 yen, and expenses for dealing — such as transportation, a rented apartment, and hotel fees — were less than 400 000 yen. Consequently, his net profit was estimated to be more than 1 million yen a month. Even though he made a sizable profit on these sales he spent much of the money on gambling, drinking, and women.

Mr. N stated that he expected to continue in the drug business for three years and planned to save 10 million yen in preparation for his eventual arrest. This included funds for buying a snack bar for his wife to support his family, funds for bail, and funds for a lawyer. He had saved 6 million yen in only six months of street-level drug dealing. In that period he did not use stimulants in order to avoid detection and arrest. One day, however, he had a quarrel with his wife and beat her, and she ran away from home. This marked the end of his self-imposed drug-free life. Wandering among various night spots with bad companions every night, he soon started gambling and using stimulants again. Six months later, he had exhausted his bank account and was becoming short of funds to buy stimulants. He was arrested shortly thereafter.

In all, Mr. N supplied 20 to 30 customers. They were mostly gang members, nightclub workers and truck drivers. As he was able to offer high-quality drugs, no "sales promotion" was needed to attract customers: they flocked to him by word of mouth. Mr. N avoided sales to addicted customers. Deals were made by phone and exchanges took place at coffee shops or on street corners after he confirmed that no suspicious person was following him. Sometimes he felt extremely anxious and imagined that he could see shadows cast by pursuers. Sometimes he felt he was on the brink of a nervous breakdown. He said dealers must be very careful in their daily activities to avoid police detection.

Since dealing late at night increased the chances of catching the attention of the police, he restricted his business to the daytime. He changed his phone number every three months and ceased relations with all his customers except the ten most reliable ones. If a customer who normally came to buy drugs every three days did not come to him for ten days, he stopped all dealing because he was afraid that the customer had been arrested and the police were watching him. He did not keep drugs in his house but rather in a suitable place near his rented apartment. A few months before his arrest, Mr. N employed a salesman and became an owner of a clandestine stimulant shop.

Interview With a Street Dealer

Mr. K, a 34 year old ex-Yakuza, was employed by Mr. N. He had a record of seven arrests and three imprisonments. A tender-looking man and smooth talker, he was also said to be a swindler. He had used stimulants, marijuana, sedatives, and glue in his youth. He had started again to use stimulants a year before, and he became a customer of Mr. N. After he came to be trusted and relied upon, he was asked to become a salesman for Mr. N.

The two opened a clandestine stimulant shop in a rented apartment and began to collect orders from customers by phone. After confirming customers through a peep hole in the door, Mr. K would hand over the drugs in exchange for cash through a chain-locked and slightly-opened door. Soon Mr. K employed a boy as an assistant to answer the phone. He then spent the daytime in pachinko parlors (a pin-ball gambling game) waiting for calls from his assistant.

They had 50 to 60 regular customers of whom one-third were Yakuza. Of the remaining two-thirds, about ten were women, half of whom were massage parlor girls. The apartment soon became well-known among neighbors for its illegal activities. Mr. N therefore told Mr. K to move the shop from that apartment to another place to forestall a police raid.

Every day, members of other gangs came to the shop to threaten Mr. K by demanding a protection fee, on two occasions injuring him by sword. In these cases, the O family, Mr. N's group, was forced to protect the business, but the family, with a majority of members incarcerated at the time, soon lost power and was unable to confront other gangs.

Mr. K dealt with approximately 20 customers each Saturday, 10 on each weekday and only a few on Sundays. His price for the drug was the same as Mr. N's price. On average he sold 14 to 15 packages a day, yielding 100 000 yen in gross income. The monthly gross income was 3 million yen, of which 1 million yen were used for buying stimulants and 500 000 yen for renting the apartment and other business expenses. Net profit was 1.5 million yen a month, divided 70% to N and 30% to K. Mr. K's income, therefore, was 450 000 yen less 100 000 yen paid to his assistant. As his occupational privilege, he himself used stimulants twice a day.

In the event of a police raid on the apartment, his plan was to dispose of the stimulants in the toilet and flush them away. When a police raid finally did occur, Mr. K successfully carried out his plan but his frightened assistant was arrested in possession of drugs.

Factors Affecting the Price of Stimulants

Table 2 clearly shows that the stimulant drug trade is extremely lucrative. One gram of stimulants may sell for 2 500 yen wholesale, but by the time it reaches the street it may retail for as much as 160 000 yen. As with any other commodity, the price is incremented at each level of the distribution system. With each step of distribution, from importer to street dealer, the price goes up enormously. The amount and quality of the drug also determine the price. At any given level of distribution, the price depends on the amount of the transaction. In large deals, prices are reduced accordingly. Naturally, high-quality drugs are higher-priced than those which have been adulterated. However, active substances are sometimes added to increase the desired effects.

Table 2   Price of Stimulant Per Gram in Each Level of the Distributon System

Level	Amount of dealing in a transaction	Average price per gram
Wholesale dealer	More than 1 kg	2 500 yen
	100 g – 1 kg	4 000 yen
Middle level dealer	10 g – 100 g	8 000 yen
	1 g – 10 g	16 000 yen
Street dealer	0.1 g – 1 g	45 000 yen
	0.05 g – 0.1 g	110 000 yen
	Less than 0.05 g	160 000 yen

(National Police Agency data, surveyed in 1987)

The relationship with a customer also affects the price. Generally, dealers sell drugs at a lower price to reliable customers and gangs with whom they are on good terms. For ordinary persons, new customers and opposing gangs, there is greater risk associated with the transaction and prices are adjusted accordingly. Also, prices differ according to regions of Japan. For example, stimulants are higher-priced in the eastern regions. The reason for such price differentials is related to the complexity and "density" of the distribution network and the distance from which drugs are imported. Where there are many users and gangsters, the distribution network becomes sufficiently dense to encourage competition and lower prices. Where law enforcement pressure is strong, the distribution network begins to break down and prices are higher to compensate for the increased risks of arrest.

Characteristics of the Stimulant Distribution Business

Government efforts to control the distribution of stimulant drugs involve a combination of increased police resources and harsher criminal sanctions. Dealers must be careful to avoid detection and arrest, for punishment in Japan can be very severe — up to life imprisonment for importers and manufacturers. Dealers therefore will go to great lengths to keep transactions secret and to minimize the number of people sharing knowledge about them.

Trafficking in stimulant drugs is an illegal activity for which dealers cannot expect official protection from the laws or police. In addition, there are always the factors of highjacking and embezzlement. Dealers require physical resources to protect themselves. Membership within the Yakuza is thus very useful, if not absolutely necessary, in the face of known risks.

An increase in business activity, while accompanied by higher profits, also means increased risk of detection and arrest. As the number of transactions and customers grows, the risk of apprehension is similarly increased. When dealers restrict the number of customers to "reliable people," their business experiences slowed growth. Street dealers who trade with many kinds of customers, including addicts, ordinary persons, and juveniles, are at higher risk than dealers at higher levels of the distribution chain who trade only with professional dealers.

As in any business, there is competition among dealers. A dealer who sells high-quality drugs at a lower price wins more customers and makes larger profits. Dealers require numerous supply routes for their drugs in order to stabilize availability, quality, and price. Making customers feel safe from the danger of detection and arrest is also a strong sales point for dealers. Sources of supply must remain secret to lower-level dealers and customers. All within the distribution chain are constantly seeking connections at higher levels to secure supplies of drugs at lower prices, skipping tiers of the distribution system whenever possible. Finally, a dealer is wise not to rely on or become overly familiar with customers.

The code of security measures practiced by drug dealers include the following:

1. *Do not use stimulants.* This is an ironclad rule for dealers, but one not easily adhered to since very often they themselves have entered the business because of using stimulants.

2. *Do not keep drugs close at hand. Conceal them in a secure place and hide all traces.* It is essential for a dealer to use reliable subordinates for actual transactions and to handle personally all matters dealing with supply and sales management.
3. *Select customers carefully. Never transact business with addicts, women, or juveniles.* All such people are considered indiscreet. A non-Yakuza is also an unreliable customer for much the same reason.
4. *Keep your identity secret. Avoid direct contact with customers.* A dealer should use a proxy, an office telephone and keep his real name and address absolutely secret.
5. *Keep a low profile and lead a modest life. Conceal business transactions under the cover of normal daily activities.* Conspicuous behavior, such as spending large sums of money in an ostentatious way, raises people's suspicions and may result in jealousy. Suspicious and jealous people may become police informants.

Although it is costly and difficult to abide by these measures, they are generally followed by dealers at the higher levels of the distribution system. It is difficult, however, for others to adhere strictly to them.

Discussion

Japan managed to achieve a rare accomplishment when it succeeded in stopping the first stimulant epidemic following World War II. The reason for this success is thought to be based on three factors.

First, the policy of criminalization enabled authorities to penalize large numbers of dealers and users and to isolate core members of the drug distribution system from the rest of society. Moreover, the threat of imprisonment made law-abiding would-be users refrain from using the drug. The result was a reduction in both supply and demand.

Second, sources of supply of the drug at that time were domestic. Supplies initially came from military stocks, later from pharmaceutical factories and clandestine domestic laboratories. The sources changed as new government drug laws were enacted. In comparison to the overseas sources that currently supply stimulant drugs to the Yakuza, domestic sources were easier to interdict.

Third, by the mid-1950s, social conditions that in the past had been conducive to the general acceptance of stimulants, had changed. In the immediate postwar era, stimulants were cheaper than alcoholic beverages and provided an easy escape for people living in a devastated and confused society. In addition, illegal transactions involving food and other necessities were daily occurrences for ordinary people. Under such conditions, purchasing drugs simply became one more illicit transaction. The government promoted a national movement for the eradication of stimulants, but this only began to have an effect when economic conditions improved and society began to stabilize.

Unlike the first epidemic, however, it seems rather difficult to put an end to the second. The Japanese are afraid that their society is gradually becoming similar to Western industrialized countries, which themselves face severe drug problems. Japan's current drug problems derive not so much from poverty and social disorder, but from affluence, alienation, and restlessness. This time around, the repeated revisions of the Stimulant Control Law, providing even more punishment for violators, have not had any apparent effect on the level of drug abuse. For one thing, co-operation with foreign law enforcement agencies is far from satisfactory, and thus it is impossible to crack down on overseas suppliers. Moreover, increased penal sanctions or campaigns against the use of stimulants are not likely to have much effect on individuals who are seeking pleasure and release to counteract the effects of a society which is affluent but also somewhat monotonous.

There also appears to be a danger of drug abuse increasing among young people. Glue sniffing has reached epidemic proportions among juveniles, and new waves of drug abuse (such as consuming sleeping pills and drinking cough syrup) are continually being reported. There is some evidence that international organizations involved in drug trafficking may be beginning to view Japan as a lucrative and promising market for their drugs. Cocaine may find a ready market in Japan, while hallucinogens might conceivably appeal to younger persons. Heroin is stockpiled in Southeast Asian countries, and suppliers are continually looking for new markets. The reason why international drug organizations have not invaded Japan can be traced to its insularity. The Japanese drug market is restricted by its ethnic homogeneity, the limited international use of the Japanese language, and the monopoloy that the Yakuza have gained in supplying stimulants. These factors constitute formidable barriers to any foreign organization seeking to enter the Japanese market.

In the final analysis, the introduction of other types of drugs into Japan depends on the Yakuza. If they conclude that other drugs will sell well in the Japanese market and they are able to make the necessary connections with international organizations, the Yakuza will start trafficking in these drugs. In contrast to the older generation of right-wing, nationalistic Yakuza, the new generation seems unlikely to hesitate over the importation of heroin if it is considered profitable. So far, heroin confiscated in Japan (4.7 kg in 1987) involves shipments that have entered the country for packing and re-shipment to the United States. Heroin is not yet generally directed at the Japanese market. However, small quantities of cocaine (1.6 kg confiscated in 1987) are thought to have been brought into Japan by international dealers to test the indigenous market.

If Yakuza organizations introduce drugs other than stimulants, users initially will be limited to Yakuza members and others influenced by the Yakuza subculture. It will probably take several years for other drugs to reach epidemic proportions as large as those of stimulants. It is probably also reasonable to state that without radical social changes affecting people's desire for drugs, the current level of drug abuse will remain unchanged.

Japan has some advantages in coping with drug problems that are not shared by Western countries. Among other things, both the general crime situation and the problem of drugs (other than stimulants) are less severe. Moreover, the number of foreign immigrants and laborers, sometimes alleged to play a role in crime and drug usage in Western countries, is quite low in Japan. In addition, Japanese family bonds are still strong and quite effective. Similarly, the police in Japan enjoy public trust and receive a great deal of co-operation and assistance. However, in recent years these factors are thought to be weakening. Among other things, the divorce rate is increasing and police corruption and malpractice are increasingly coming to the public's attention.

On the other hand, the Japanese public does seem willing to surrender some of its individual rights for the sake of collective security. This tendency can be seen in a recent amendment to the road traffic control law that provides increased sanctions for drunk driving. Even though Japan is quite tolerant as regards alcohol consumption, the regulations are accepted because people feel the public's safety is more important than the individual's right to drive when impaired by abuse of alcohol. In such a moral climate, it is possible to enact laws strictly controlling the dealers and users of drugs for the good of the general public.

In some Western countries, the decriminalization of drug abuse has become a controversial issue among researchers, politicians, and the public. In Japan, however, the decriminalization of drugs is thought to be an unrealistic solution of the problem and no politician, law enforcement offical, or reseacher seriously advocates this approach.

There are a number of reasons why decriminalization is unlikely to be adopted in Japan. First, the Japanese think that the general law enforcement system is functioning well and feel no real need to change it. Second, Japanese drug abuse has not reached unconscionable levels. Stimulant use is still largely limited to the Yakuza and the lower classes. Decriminalization would merely exacerbate the problem and put it beyond the control of the authorities. The situation would be comparable to the days before criminalization was introduced to control the first wave of stimulant abuse. Third, approximately half of those arrested for violations of the Stimulant Control Law belong to the Yakuza or are peripheral members, and some 80% of the people arrested have previous arrest records. As a result, the general public lacks sympathy for people who use stimulants. Fourth, although the Stimulant Control Law may provide for severe penalties for violators, in actual practice the penalties are applied flexibly. First-time offenders, non-criminal infrequent users and those who have a strong desire to quit the habit are likely to escape with a fine, probation, or suspended sentence. Japan, therefore, is likely to continue to adopt increasingly severe drug control policies. As a matter of course, the main target of the law enforcement efforts is the Yakuza. However, so long as the Yakuza organizations manage to maintain their present membership numbers and sources of income, no real solution to the problem exists.

Conclusion

The most efficient measure for drug control is to crack down on the source of drugs and eliminate those at the peak of the distribution system. In order to crack down on the overseas supply of stimulants, co-operation with foreign law enforcement agencies is essential. The Japanese National Police Agency has been conducting a regular international seminar on control of narcotic offenses, inviting participants from South East Asia and other countries. There are also regular meetings with American officials to exchange information on organized crime. In addition to this, Japan has supplied other Asian police forces with sophisticated tools for chemical analysis, as well as other forms of police equipment. Even software for drug traffic control and crime prevention systems has been supplied (see Bayley, 1976). Given the mutual understanding that has emerged out of official conferences and exchanges of support, it should be possible to develop a sufficient level of international co-operation to allow for a smooth exchange of information, the arrest of fugitives, and the elimination of clandestine laboratories in other countries.

As for domestic measures against importers, usually senior members of Yakuza organizations, information gathering is a most important tool. We have to consider seriously the introduction of covert investigative activities such as wiretapping, controlled deliveries and sting operations, all of which are generally prohibited by Japanese law today.

To reduce the human resources of Yakuza organizations, dealers and users who are members of the Yakuza must be arrested and incapacitated for as long as the law allows. This strategy has already been undertaken by the police, as was shown in the interview with Mr. N, a middle-level dealer.

In addition, some effort must be put into reducing the income of the Yakuza. One possible tool is checking for tax evasion among individual members. It is difficult to detect income that mainly comes from illegal activities, but if successful it would be a heavy blow to the Yakuza. Further examination of this strategy and the co-operation of tax agencies are necessary to put it into practice.

Control of the Yakuza ultimately depends on the co-operation of the average citizen. Some think the Yakuza are a necessary evil and use them for solving problems with others. Others do not want to make accusations against Yakuza members because they fear retaliation. To change such attitudes, police have to establish ways of protecting people from the Yakuza and to foster a civil movement against them. In some areas, such civil movements already have been successful in driving the Yakuza from the communities. This has involved repeated protest activities and long-term surveillance of Yakuza headquarters. Extensive mass media coverage of such operations is essential for developing public support.

References

Bayley, David, H. 1976. *Forces of Order: Police Behavior in Japan and the United States.* Berkeley and Los Angeles, CA: University of California Press.

Fukushima, Akira. 1977. "Stimulant Abuse: Its Psychopathology and Criminal Responsibility." in *A Study on Criminal Psychology* 1(in Japanese). Tokyo: Kongo Shuppan Publishers pp. 9-27.

Ministry of Justice. 1988. *The White Paper on Crime, 1987.* (in Japanese).

National Police Agency. 1981. *Statistics on Stimulant and Other Drug Offenses in 1980* (in Japanese).

———. 1988a. *White Paper on Police, 1988* (in Japanese).

———. 1988b. *Statistics on Stimulant and Other Drug Offenses in 1987* (in Japanese).

Tamura, Masayuki. 1982. "Methamphetamine Epidemic and Law Enforcement." *Japanese Journal of Sociological Criminology.* No.7. pp. 4-32. (in Japanese)

Tamura, Masayuki. 1983. "International Drug Traffic and Stimulants in Japan." Hanzai to Hikou *(Journal of Crime and Delinquency).* No. 57. pp. 75-105. (in Japanese)

Tatetsu, Seijun, Akio Goto and Tsuyoshi Fujiwara. 1956. *The Methamphetamine Psychosis* (in Japanese). Tokyo: Igaku Shoin Ltd.

7

The Organized Crime/Drug Connection: National and International Perspectives

Ernesto Ugo Savona

The social alarm surrounding drug trafficking and organized crime comprises both a risk and a merit. The risk is that the focus on drug trafficking *per se* will cause us to overlook the fact that it is but one aspect of organized crime. The merit is that drug trafficking is becoming the main factor underlying changes in the organization of crime groups. These points can be reconciled, though, by considering drug trafficking within the broader context of changes in organized crime.

Successful drug market operations require organizational structures different from those in other illegal activities such as gambling or loansharking. Drug traffickers need to carry out international activities, and they must have a monopolistic position in at least one of the crucial segments of the market (production, processing, smuggling, and distribution).

International drug operations have traditionally developed along a migratory path. Ethnic links have characterized Chinese heroin traffic, for example, from production in Southeast Asia (where Chinese organized crime groups maintain a monopoly) to distribution through Chinese residents in consumer countries such as the United States. Similarly, international links and operations were necessary for the Colombian drug cartels to develop control of the cocaine market. The Colombian cartels buy virtually the entire coca leaf crop of Bolivia, Peru, and Columbia and process it into cocaine which is smuggled into the U.S. and Europe. Intermediate level distribution in these countries is handled by networks of Columbian residents (U.S. General Accounting Office, 1989).

The thesis that international connections are essential to entering the drug market is supported by the fact that well-established La Cosa Nostra criminal organizations in the U.S. have been unable to enter the drug market on the same scale as other illegal markets.[1] In contrast, the Sicilian Mafia has controlled much of the American heroin market since the 1960s by following routes of immigration to the U.S. from the Middle East. A large number of Sicilian *mafiosi* entered the U.S. during the early 1960s, establishing a nucleus of Sicilian Mafia in America, the so-called "Sicilian Connection" which, during the 1970s and early 1980s, acted as an intermediary in processing and shipping heroin between the producing countries in the Middle East and the U.S.[2]

Internationalization is an adaptation some multi-task criminal organizations have developed in order to enter drug markets. It can also be considered as the starting point for emerging drug trafficking organizations, now single-tasked but which may become multi-tasked in the future. Traditional criminal groups have often followed the path of differentiation along a continuum from illegal markets to legal ones. The Colombian drug cartels, increasing in wealth and power, will almost certainly follow the same path (Smith, 1980). Further, the drug cartels' international connections will allow them to carry out new operations on a global scale. All of these elements call for a strategy against organized crime in which national and international perspectives are combined and crime control is integrated with other forms of regulatory processes.

This chapter contains an analysis of the national and international dimensions of organized crime with particular reference to drug trafficking. The structures and activities of different organized crime groups will be analyzed to consider the most effective strategies by which to control them.

The Evolution of Organized Crime

There are signs of a transformation in the nature of criminality that enable one to speculate on the development of a process of rationalization of criminality. This process follows the trend toward more organizational complexity characterizing modern societies. This transformation may be observed in a variety of countries, both developed and developing, with different political systems. The process of rationalization implies a complicated reorganization on the part of crime groups following enterprise patterns increasingly capable of controlling a vast spectrum of illegal and legal activities (Savona, 1990).

This process will probably have a profound effect on the nature of crime in coming years. New developments within the process can be seen in the functional interdependence increasingly linking traditionally separate areas of criminality. Street crime (violence and theft), political crime, and organized crime are all increasingly drawn into the rationalization process.

A clear example of the way in which the rationalization of criminality produces and links different forms of crime can be found in the area of drugs. Organizations operating at different levels produce corruption and violence against law enforcement officials and against competitive organizations. They launder and reinvest their illegal proceeds, and indirectly solicit drug users to commit other crimes — burglaries, robberies, and thefts — to generate the income needed to obtain the illegal drugs.

To better understand the differences between non-organized and organized crime, a broad dynamic concept of "organization of crime" is adopted here. Different levels of organization of crime produce differently structured groups. Two useful criteria for distinguishing organized crime groups from non-organized ones are "durability and reputation."[3]

It is impossible to gather under a definitional umbrella the many different structures of organized crime groups that vary by ethnic origins, market opportunities, and other factors. A descriptive distinction between "traditional" and "nontraditional" organized crime is frequently used in the U.S. to distinguish groups such as La Cosa Nostra from other groups such as Colombian drug organizations, Jamaican Posses, Chinese and Vietnamese gangs, or Los Angeles street gangs (U.S. General Accounting Office, 1989).

These and many other similar groups have sometimes been called "new" or "emerging" groups. Yet, rather than indicating the history of each group, they actually refer to the varying degrees of attention law enforcement agencies have paid to different organized crime groups in the past. In this framework, Chinese organized crime, with very old origins, is considered "emerging" because it has only recently received attention from law enforcement agencies.

Organizational Structures and Activities

Analysis of the different structures that organized groups present is useful in planning effective control strategies. Traditional approaches to prosecuting and convicting individual members of organized groups have not been very effective; vacancies are quickly filled by new recruits. New law enforcement approaches define organized crime groups as business enterprises, and are developing a broad range of actions to eliminate them.

There are many conflicting opinions about the organizational structure of what is considered traditional organized crime. In the U.S., the federal government's official position, reinforced by research conducted with official records (Cressey, 1969), describes La Cosa Nostra as a number of "families" or hierarchical organizations whose members are of Italian origin and which have for some time been closely linked in a syndicate ("Commission"). A similar structure has been recently demonstrated for the Italian Mafia at the conclusion of the trial of 474 *mafiosi*. Other researchers consider these groups to be less organized than is indicated in official records (Ianni, 1974), seeing them mainly as criminal networks or patron-client relationships (Albini, 1971). The available data, however, suggest the "organized/disorganized" model is simplistic. Research carried out on single activities such as gambling has shown that the structures of traditional organized groups change over time according to their activity and the locations in which they operate (Reuter, 1983).

Traditional organized crime groups are territorially connected. They act mainly at a local/national level. The partial involvement in the heroin trade by some traditional organized crime groups in the U.S. and Europe has made it necessary for them to operate on an international level. The "French Connection" (until the mid-1970s), the "Pizza Connection" (from the late 1970s until the early 1980s), and the recent "Iron Tower" operation of 1988 are the international links between European-based groups and American ones.

The different requirements and specialties connected with drug markets have internationalized crime groups. Production, smuggling, distribution (at both intermediate and street levels), and the laundering of cash and its investment in illegal and legal activities have multiplied and diversified the organizational structures of groups operating in the drug markets. Some of these groups can be considered organized crime groups because they have the characteristics of durability and reputation.

Such groups are often involved with at least one of the different links in the chain that connects drug supply with demand. The heroin market has traditionally involved criminal organizations in the protection of poppy cultivation, as well as in the manufacture and distribution of heroin. Each or several of these stages is controlled by one or more groups. The opium poppy is grown in many areas of the world and this has increased competition among groups acting at different stages. The market can be seen as two funnels connected at their spouts with more groups in the terminal phases of production and distribution and almost monopolistic structures in the intermediate phase of heroin manufacture. This step has been traditionally controlled by a few powerful organized groups, among them the Sicilian Mafia.

Increased demand for cocaine and the limited areas where coca leaves are cultivated (mostly in Peru, Bolivia and, to a lesser degree, Colombia) have allowed the development of a constellation of organized crime groups that have recently attracted national and international attention. The four Colombian drug cartels are the result of a well organized division of labor in the cocaine market. They buy almost the entire production of coca leaves from Bolivia and Peru, and manufacture and smuggle cocaine through different routes to the consumer countries where they control its intermediate distribution. Each cartel is composed of independent trafficking organizations which, for reasons of efficiency, act in the market in a coordinated way. Competition exists among the different cartels for control of sections of the market. The Colombian drug cartels maintain networks in the U.S. and are developing other networks elsewhere. At times they operate in connection with other criminal organizations for smuggling or distribution purposes. The cartels have monopolized the cocaine market except for the street trade.

This market can be seen as a pyramid with the cartels at the apex (monopoly) and many competing criminal organizations at the base (free enterprise).

Organized crime groups have migrated from Asia to other parts of the world. The oldest and most structured Chinese criminal organizations are the Hong Kong-based Triads, multi-task organizations that have evolved from secret societies formed in the seventeenth century to overthrow the Ching Dynasty. Many of the old rituals, such as initiation, are still observed (Bresler, 1980; Morgan, 1960). Some of the Triads, such as the Sun Yee On (the largest Triad society in Hong Kong) operate in countries such as the U.S., Canada, and Australia. Their drug trafficking, loansharking, and extortion activities are gradually shifting from Hong Kong to these countries in anticipation of 1997 when the People's Republic of China will assume sovereignty over Hong Kong. Triads are only a fraction of the constellation of Chinese organized crime groups operating throughout the world. In some cases there is growing evidence of joint criminal ventures between Chinese Triads and other Chinese gangs operating in Western countries such as the U.S.

The Yakuza may be the largest organized crime group in the world with almost 110 000 members and 2500 associated gangs (President's Commission, 1986). This group originated between the sixteenth and seventeenth centuries in Japan, and has evolved through hierarchical structures similar to those of the Sicilian Mafia. The *wakato* (chairman) controls several deputies, and beneath them are lieutenants who manage numerous *wakai shu* (soldiers). The social and economic changes in Japan after World War II opened many opportunities to organized crime (National Police Agency of Japan, 1983). Yakuza organizations are involved in pornography, narcotics, and extortion. They smuggle amphetamines from the U.S. to Japan and provide firearms to the highly restricted Japanese market (Los Angeles Police Department, 1984).

The groups just described represent the more important and acknowledged organized crime groups operating at the international level. Other groups of different ethnic origins can be included. They can be single- or multi-task organizations involving illicit goods and services such as drugs, gambling, and the disposal of toxic wastes.

Organized crime operate in legal markets as well. Organized crime groups infiltrate these markets, acting illegally through the exercise of corruption and violence to maximize their income. Freight cartage, waterfront, and construction industries are some examples of these activities (Reuter, Rubenstein, and Wynn, 1983; Reuter, 1987b). Other activities are currently infiltrated by organized crime groups in order to improve the groups' image and to make legally productive the money obtained through illegal activities.

Many hypotheses have been proposed about the evolution of organized crime groups, and the changes in their organizational structures and activities. References are made to socio-demographic changes that have influenced the cultural values of the group members. Values such as *omerta* (secrecy), together with narrow criteria of recruitment, characterize many different groups and their evolution.[4] There are no fixed rules to explain the market preferences of these groups. Many traditional illegal activities such as extortion, gambling, and prostitution have been dominated by different groups of varying ethnic origins. Involvement in the drug market has accelerated the general trend of changes already occurring within different organized groups and in the relationships between groups, changing what can be called the "social organization of organized crime." Individuals who are not organized crime members *per se*, such as accountants, lawyers, bank employees, chemists and airplane pilots, have connections with organized crime groups. Some of them have been the weak links in the organized crime chain. When discovered, they have frequently co-operated with law enforcement agencies.

The markets for different drugs have been instrumental in transforming the traditional structure of organized crime groups. Reaction to law enforcement policies has increased the level of violence and corruption against external targets such as police, judges, and political figures. The fragmentation of some markets, such as the street-level cocaine market, has increased competition and turnover in the territories controlled, spreading violence in its wake.

The internationalization process that characterizes some traditional and emerging groups can be understood as a combination of the socio-demographic changes within the groups and changes within market structures. A third explanation can be offered. This considers internationalization as the reaction of organized crime groups to powerful legislation and law enforcement policies enacted in some countries. These crime groups have, for example, developed money laundering schemes in order to minimize the risks and the costs of these laws and enforcement policies.

The Need for a Strategy

Organized criminal groups have reacted to the effectiveness of legislation and law enforcement policies by developing more sophisticated techniques. In fact, their evolution has surpassed the present capabilities of individual countries to effect control. It is now necessary to revise the general strategy against organized crime. This proposed strategy has a theoretical framework, prevention and control functions, acts at national and international levels, and relies on a variety of means.

Rhetoric on the subject of organized crime is proportional to the social alarm it has provoked in recent times. At national levels the connections between organized crime and political and economic interests have sometimes obstructed the adoption of effective control policies. Even where policies have been adopted, bureaucracy and competition between law enforcement agencies have weakened their implementation. Criminal organizations have used violence, fear, and corruption to maximize their profits and minimize their costs.

At the national level, societal reactions to organized crime can be positioned along a continuum ranging from maximum tolerance to maximum social control. Huge quantities of "dirty" money have found hospitality in the financial systems of countries considered financial secrecy havens. While some countries have simply ignored the problem, others have reacted by changing their laws and improving law enforcement policies. Nevertheless, many countries have ignored the importance of prevention through new regulatory policies.

International efforts have met with difficulties. Yet, some progress has been made. Recommendations, conventions, bilateral and multilateral treaties of extradition, and judicial assistance have been recently developed. Intervention in organized crime matters at the international level marks the beginning of a tentative strategy that must be developed further.

The Theoretical Framework

The growing rationalization of modern criminality demands a recognition of the need for an increasingly rational response on the part of societies' systems of social control. Rhetoric must be replaced by rational choices adopted at both the national and international level. A useful guide to such change can be the economic analysis of organized crime, which can be used as a basis to develop policies that counter the problems created by organized crime (Schelling, 1980). Such a strategy entails choices directly related to the specific problems posed by organized crime (Savona, 1987). The choices must be sought within an integrated strategy that combines preventive policies with control policies. In the area of prevention, new regulatory policies must be considered for those markets (legal or illegal) in which organized crime groups try to develop monopolies. In the area of control, policies must be developed to assist law enforcement agencies eradicate organized crime.

Preventive Policies

Preventive policies can be of many kinds: social, economic, and educational. Their goal is to change the conditions that foster organized crime's development. Necessary distinctions must be made, though, for different kinds of industries. One such distinction must be between legal and illegal markets. Reducing the susceptibility to racketeering of some legal industries can deter infiltration by organized crime groups.[5] This can be accomplished through regulatory policies that change the structure of opportunities within these industries.

However, such policies do not work vis-a-vis illegal markets. Consequently, they cannot be used to sever the link between organized crime and drugs. For illegal markets, the following preventive policies can be considered:
(1) legalization;
(2) policies directed at the reduction of demand for illegal goods or services (in the case of drugs, education policies intended to prevent drug abuse or sanctions imposed on drug users as a deterrent);
(3) policies to prevent the use of illicit profits, particularly their investment in legal commerce; and
(4) firearms regulation.

Legalization and demand reduction aim to reduce organized crime's involvement in drugs. The former achieves this result by eliminating the added value that drugs acquire due to their illegal status, the latter by reducing the number of buyers and, in turn, the incentive of sellers. These policies produce different consequences. While the legalization hypothesis can only be evaluated on the basis of theoretical scenarios (see Galliher, Chapter 9), the demand reduction hypothesis is widely accepted. Recent international research concludes that reducing demand is the key issue.[6] Many countries are trying to reduce drug demand by increasing penalties for users. The results of these policies, however, have not been encouraging.

A third preventive policy refers to what is generally called "money laundering." Two international reports that address this issue from different viewpoints are the report of the United Nations Convention against Illicit Traffic in Narcotic Drugs and Psychotropic Substances of 1988 and the Statement of the Principles of the Committee on Banking Regulations and Supervisory Practices. The international community is confronted with the difficult task of maximizing the free flow of capital within and between national borders while minimizing the risks of illicitly earned money circulating within financial institutions. Weak regulatory policies allow dirty money to avoid taxation and to be laundered and invested. In this area, there are many options for discouraging countries that consciously compete to attract illicit funds and for exercising preventive control on the circulation of such money. The following are necessary measures: (1) harmonizing the laws of different countries with regard to the amount of money that can be freely moved, (2) deciding when bank secrecy cannot be allowed to obstruct law enforcement, and (3) organizing data base systems at the national level with international links programmed to alert authorities regarding suspicious financial transactions.[7]

Another important area that cuts across national and international boundaries is the regulation of firearms. In some countries it is easy to buy firearms of every kind; in others it is much more difficult. The international dimensions of crime make it possible for some organized groups to buy firearms legally in the U.S. and use them against competitors or public officials in the U.S. or other countries. The irony of this dangerous deregulation is that some powerful organized groups, such as the Colombian drug cartels, have formed private armies and supplied them with sophisticated weapons legally purchased abroad.

Criminal Control Policies

A first rough distinction can be drawn between countries with and without specific legislation targeting organized crime and drug trafficking. Many other distinctions can be made between the substantive provisions and between the penalties provided by these laws. The types of conduct considered criminal fall within the following typology:

a) using or investing income derived from a pattern of racketeering activity to acquire an enterprise engaged in or affecting commerce;

b) acquiring an interest in such an enterprise through a pattern of racketeering activity;

c) conducting the affairs of an enterprise through a pattern of racketeering activity;

d) conspiring to commit any of the first three violations.

New criminal penalties beyond fines and imprisonment provide for the forfeiture and seizure of the economic products of illegal activity. Some laws provide for civil remedies which, as in the U.S., (1) include but are not limited to ordering any person to divest himself of any interest, direct or indirect, in any enterprise; (2) impose reasonable restrictions on the future activities or investments of any person, including, but not limited to, prohibiting engagement in the same type of endeavor as the enterprise engaged in which affect interstate or foreign commerce; or (3) mandate the dissolution or reorganization of any enterprise. In the U.S. these remedies are issued by federal district courts mainly in the area of labor racketeering and corruption (Giuliani, 1987). Many differences in criminal procedures can be found among societies. The two models of trial, accusatorial and inquisitorial, present advantages and disadvantages in prosecuting organized crime cases. Usually organized crime matters have been considered problems of substantive law, thus neglecting the important role played by procedural law in this area. The nearly impenetrable organization of criminal groups, abetted by skilled lawyers, add to the problems faced by prosecutors in bringing strong evidence to court. Success in prosecuting organized crime cases depends mainly on the skill of the agencies in gathering intelligence and conducting investigations. New models for intelligence gathering are required. And new incentives are needed to encourage better co-ordination among law enforcement agencies.

The entrepreneurial pattern followed by organized crime groups has changed the intelligence activity used against them. The intelligence process involves four steps, the end product of which is the transformation of raw data into what is commonly called "finished intelligence." The first of these steps is the collection of raw information. Information is collected in accordance with one or more hypotheses from a variety of sources including informants, co-operative witnesses, and electronic surveillance. This information is then evaluated for its consistency with data collected through other sources. The data are thereafter organized around specific categories such as crime activities, geographic territories, and *modus operandi*. Finally, the data are analyzed and interpreted in terms of either immediate enforcement response, called tactical intelligence, or long-term enforcement response, called strategic intelligence (Martens, 1987; Godfrey and Harris, 1971). Tactical intelligence can produce immediate results in terms of the prosecution of individuals, while strategic intelligence devoted to the understanding of the enterprise structure and activities can lead to the dissolution of the criminal organizations.

Organized crime investigations are often characterized by a high level of conflict between different agencies. At times, the production of immediate results is preferred to long-term investigation that is more effective in terms of enforcement but less effective in terms of visibility. In order to improve the effectiveness and efficiency of the investigative process it is necessary to avoid agency conflicts. Co-ordination is an extremely important element of an integrated strategy targeting organized crime. Positive results have been achieved in those countries whose different law enforcement agencies have worked together to form "strike forces" at different levels of jurisdiction.

In many countries, co-operative witnesses have successfully contributed to the prosecution and conviction of organized crime members. Various reasons may lead a member of an organized crime group or someone connected with the organized crime group to co-operate with law enforcement agencies. Experience indicates that these reasons fall into two main categories: (1) conflicts between the member and the organization to which he or she belongs, and (2) pressure arising from evidence of his or her membership in the organized crime group. Both situations produce a conflict between self-interest and loyalty to the organization. In the former, co-operation is exchanged for protection by law enforcement agencies; in the latter, co-operation is exchanged for the promise of a reduced penalty. The decision to solicit the witness' co-operation (and the consequent bargaining) can be considered contradictory to equity of the law. This is an example of the trade-off between efficiency and equity within the criminal justice system. Nevertheless, fostering such cooperation is an effective instrument for gathering of evidence against organized crime groups and for avoiding the risk of acquittal that has often accompanied organized crime trials.

Conclusion

If the organized crime-drug connection has changed the nature of organized crime, it is also changing the way criminal justice systems react to the phenomenon, and it must change the way policy makers and practitioners think about it. Though awareness of the international dimensions of the problem has grown, it has not yet yielded a sufficiently rational approach.

The traditional strategy used to combat organized crime is to combine specific criminal laws directed at organized crime activities and entities together with aggressive law enforcement policies. When this strategy has been applied, as for example against La Cosa Nostra in the U.S., it has resulted in many convictions of individual members but little reduction in illegal activities. A number of explanations have been put forward to explain this. One is that younger members of La Cosa Nostra have filled the leadership voids left by convictions. Another is that other organized groups have entered activities traditionally controlled by La Cosa Nostra.

If a conclusion can be drawn from these results, it is that criminal sanctions alone are ineffective. Their effects on criminal organizations are limited. A better alternative would be for law enforcement to concentrate on following the money trail. The investigation of money laundering and the confiscation of proceeds derived from criminal activities powerfully impact the main task of criminal organizations: the production of wealth. The success of this strategy will depend on international co-operation and the resolve of governments to open their financial affairs to greater scrutiny.

Notes

1. This is a personal interpretation, contrary to the general assumption that La Cosa Nostra have refrained from entering the drug markets. The fact that many La Cosa Nostra members have been convicted for drug charges, mainly at low levels in the heroin market, and the apparent non-involvement of La Cosa Nostra in the cocaine market confirms that the decision not to enter the market was for La Cosa Nostra a question of perceived inability to operate within the markets' structures.

2. Italian and American law enforcement sources estimate that the 70% of the heroin entering the U.S. come through Sicilian connections (McWeeny, 1987:5).

3. Reuter states durability ". . . might be determined by identification of a generational change in leadership without loss of continuity." He defines reputation ". . . as an extrinsic variable . . . a knowledge of the existence, and a belief in the powers, of the gang held by others" (Reuter, 1987a:179).

4. Statement of Ronald Goldstock on the parallels between Sicilian and American Mafia and Chinese Triads (President's Commission on Organized Crime, 1984:283).

5. Racketeering susceptibility is intended as the degree to which an industry's structure and organization create incentives for participants to engage in racketeering or provide the means and opportunity for racketeers both within and outside the industry to control or influence critical industry components (Goldstock, 1990).

6. See the Adoption of a Political Declaration and a Global Program of Action, 70th Special Session of the General Assembly of the United Nations, New York, February 20-23, 1990, (Document A/S-17/11, March 26, 1990), and Declaration of the World Ministerial Summit to Reduce Demand for Drugs and to Combat the Cocaine Threat, London, April 9-11, 1990.

7. See the recommendations provided in the report of the Financial Action Task Force on Money Laundering, Paris, February 1990.

References

Albini, Joseph L. 1971. *The American Mafia: Genesis of a Legend*. New York: Appleton-Century-Crofts.

Bresler, Fenton. 1980. *The Chinese Mafia*. New York: Stein and Day.

Cressey, Donald R. 1969. *Theft of the Nation*. New York: Harper and Row.

Giuliani, Rudolph. 1987. "Legal Remedies for Attacking Organized Crime," pp. 103-130, in Herbert Edelhertz (ed.), *Major Issues in Organized Crime Control*. Washington, D. C.: National Institute of Justice.

Godfrey, E. Drexel, Jr. and Don R. Harris. 1971. *Basic Elements of Intelligence*. Washington, D. C.: Law Enforcement Assistance Administration.

Goldstock, Ronald. 1990. "Beyond Criminal Sanctions," paper presented at a panel discussion on The Struggle Against Organized Crime and Drugs: An Evaluation of the American Experience, Blair House, Washington, D. C.

Ianni, Francis A. J. 1974. *Black Mafia: Ethnic Succession in Organized Crime.* New York: Simon and Schuster.

Los Angeles Police Department. 1984. *Report on the Yakuza.* Los Angeles: Organized Crime Intelligence Division, Los Angeles Police Department.

Martens, Frederick T. 1987. "The Intelligence Function," pp. 131-151, in Herbert Edelhertz (ed.), *Major Issues in Organized Crime Control.* Washington, D. C.: National Institute of Justice.

McWeeny, Sean M. 1987. "Sicilian Mafia and its Impact on the United States," *FBI Law Enforcement Bulletin* 56: 1-10.

Morgan, W. P. 1960. *Triad Societies in Hong Kong.* Hong Kong: Hong Kong Government Printer.

National Police Agency of Japan. 1983. *White Paper on Police.* Tokyo: Okurasho Insatsu-kyoku.

President's Commission on Organized Crime. 1984. *Organized Crime of Asian Origin.* Washington, D. C.: Government Printing Office.

———. 1986. *The Impact: Organized Crime Today.* Washington, D. C.: Government Printing Office.

Reuter, Peter. 1983. *Disorganized Crime.* Cambridge, MA: M.I.T. Press.

———. 1987a. "Methodological Problems of Organized Crime Research," pp. 169-189, in Herbert Edelhertz (ed.), *Major Issues in Organized Crime Control,* Washington, D. C.: National Institute of Justice.

———. 1987b. *Racketeering in Legitimate Industries.* Washington, D. C.: Rand Corporation/National Institute of Justice.

Reuter, Peter, Jonathan Rubinstein and Simon Wynn. 1983. *Racketeering in Legitimate Industries: Two Case Studies.* Washington, D. C.: National Institute of Justice.

Savona, Ernesto Ugo. 1987. "Strafrechtssystem und organisiertes Verbrechen," *Soziologisches Jarbuch* 3:287-297.

———. 1990. "Social Change, Organized Crime, and Criminal Justice System," in U. Zvetich (ed.), *Essays in Development and Crime,* Rome: UNICRI.

Schelling, Thomas C. 1980. "Economics and Criminal Enterprise," pp. 377-394, in Ralph Andreano and John J. Siegfried (eds.), *The Economics of Crime,* New York: John Wiley and Sons,

Smith, Dwight C. 1980. "Paragons, Pariahs, and Pirates: A Spectrum-Based Theory of Enterprise," *Crime and Delinquency* 26:358-386.

U. S. General Accounting Office. 1989. *Non-Traditional Organized Crime: Law Enforcement Officials' Perspectives of Five Criminal Groups.* Report to the Chairman, Permanent Subcommittee on Investigations, U. S. Senate Committee on Governmental Affairs.

8

Colonial Relations and Opium Control Policy in Hong Kong, 1841-1945

Harold H. Traver

Most research on the relationship between law and the economic and social conditions from which it emerges has been confined to Western societies. Notable exceptions to this generalization include Fitzpatrick (1980), Sumner (1982), and Huggins (1985), whose studies present detailed analyses of the role of law in maintaining control of cheap and compliant labor in Third World countries. Nevertheless, there is a relative paucity of research on other types of law in these societies. Drug laws are a case in point. Research on the creation of these laws has generally concentrated on the U.S. (Musto, 1973; Lindesmith, 1959, 1965), and particularly as they apply to marijuana in that country (Becker, 1963; Dickson, 1968; Galliher and Walker, 1976; Bonnie and Whitebread, 1974; Reasons, 1974). However, there is reason to believe that research on the origin and development of drug laws in other types of societies may yield insights into how such laws emerge in differing political and economic conditions.

This chapter examines the Hong Kong government's efforts to raise revenue from the retail sale of opium within the colony itself. In achieving this goal, the government assumed near total control over domestic consumption by the turn of the twentieth century.

For reasons that will become apparent, opium legislation was not directed at the opium trade with China or the large trading companies that controlled this trade. Instead, legislation was specifically confined to controlling the retail sale of opium within the confines of the colony in order to raise revenue from its sale.

Since 1945, however, Hong Kong has adopted an increasingly punitive stance to drug trafficking, to the point that its legal strictures are now among the harshest in the world. This chapter attempts to answer the question: How did the definition of the problem change from one of how to secure and protect an important source of government revenue to one of how to suppress domestic drug use?

Establishing Hong Kong Government's Opium Monopoly

Political states have an interest in maintaining conditions conducive to their long-term survival. Finding an adequate and reliable source of revenue is basic to this end, and Hong Kong's colonial government has pursued this goal assiduously since its founding. Of the various options available to the young colony, taxing the opium trade with China was deemed one of the most promising. Although objections were raised in some quarters concerning Britain's involvement in "so discreditable a traffic" (Colonial Records Office, 1843:73), the major obstacle was that Hong Kong had been declared a free port in 1841 and thus tariffs, a traditional way for governments to raise revenue, were unavailable. Moreover, notwithstanding its free-port status, it would have been both politically and technically difficult to seek to derive revenue from the colony's opium trade with China. The trade was Hong Kong's *raison d'etre*, and was controlled by a few large trading firms with strong political support in the United Kingdom. To interfere with their activities would have threatened the very foundations of the colony. The colonial government therefore turned to internal business activities, the only other available source of revenue.

In 1844, the British Colonial Office first raised the possibility of deriving revenue from the sale of opium. Later that year the Hong Kong Legislative Council,[1] having resolved that revenue could be derived from opium without injuring internal commerce, passed the colony's first ordinance (No. 21 of 1844) establishing a government monopoly over the retail sale of opium (Parliamentary Papers, 1971:344).[2] The ordinance authorized the colonial government to grant, on the basis of a competitive bid, a legal monopoly to sell raw and prepared opium in amounts less than one chest. The opium monopoly, or as it was called at that time, "farm," was let for one year during which time the person who had purchased the monopoly, or "farmer," had complete discretion in setting opium's retail price. Furthermore, the ordinance made it a criminal offense for anyone to possess opium that had not been bought from the farmer. The farmer was authorized to hire non-government "customs agents" to board vessels and enter dwellings for confiscation of contraband opium.

Questions were soon raised in both London and Hong Kong concerning the moral and political implications of taxing opium. The moral objections were dismissed by the Governor of Hong Kong, Sir John Davis, on the grounds that the administration classed opium "with spirits [alcohol] and such other unnecessary stimulants . . . [and] therefore does not hesitate . . . to raise a tax from the consumption of opium within the Colony" (Parliamentary Papers, 1971:344). The political questions posed by the policy of taxing opium while China adamantly refused to legalize it were likewise dismissed by Sir John who noted that the British and Chinese governments had a "perfect understanding" that both countries should adopt their own laws concerning opium.

Compared to the opium trade with China, the local retail trade was minor, yet it assumed an important role in the general economy of Hong Kong. In theory, the sale of opium should have been a reliable source of government income. However, during the three years of its operation, the revenue from opium was far less than that derived from liquor licenses. This failure can be traced to two factors: first, the ready availability of illicit opium, and second, a fundamental conflict of interest between the opium farmer and the colonial government. While the government expected the proceeds from the opium farm to support an ever-expanding administration, the opium farmer was concerned principally with maximizing the return on his investment. Achieving this meant charging the highest prices the market would sustain and, when the occasion demanded, rigging the bidding to lower the price of the farm, or flooding the market with prepared opium just prior to the farm's expiration.

The local business community's reaction to the government's auctioning of a legal monopoly on opium was swift and intense. Government policy became the object of severe criticism in the local press and, ultimately, in the British Parliament. Criticism was both ideological and practical. In the decades following the loss of the American colonies, the mercantilist ideas underlying British colonialism became largely discredited. Consequently, the new breed of British trader entering the China trade was more interested in establishing a commercial empire than a political one. These traders were therefore quite naturally disinclined to look favorably on any form of trade protection.

Hong Kong had been founded on the optimistic assumption that the China trade would expand greatly once China agreed, in the Treaty of Nanking, to a free trade policy. However, by the latter half of the 1840s it was obvious that the China trade was not expanding as expected. Thus efforts to find sources of internal revenue coincided with a general downturn of Hong Kong's economy. Among the many explanations for this failure was the allegation that the opium farmer was using his license in a manner that contributed to a reluctance on the part of Chinese junks to trade with Hong Kong. Before the colonial government established a legal monopoly on opium, junks from China would come to Hong Kong loaded with commodities and return with opium for the Chinese market. After 1844, however, these junks began to bypass Hong Kong and to conduct their trading in nearby Chinese territory to avoid Hong Kong regulations. The solution to this problem was seen by the business community to lie in an overall reduction of government regulations and expenditure. According to this view, the only acceptable form of revenue was to be derived from the sale of land leases.

Colonial officials and leading members of Hong Kong's business class clashed on the matter of the colony's future and specifically on the issue of raising government revenue. The government's need for revenue to support a growing civil service was clearly at odds with the interests of large segments of the business class. In essence, the question was whether the state existed to serve the needs of the British merchant or to promote its own interests as well. Local businessmen adopted the convenient position that Hong Kong was not "really" a colony owing to its inability to assume financial independence, and that it was properly to be seen as a place of political security and the "seat of English government in China" (Select Committee, 1847:180). If such was the case, it followed that Hong Kong should be viewed as a necessary part of the British embassy in China, a cost "which ought to be borne by the nation" (Select Committee, 1847:180). In short, the main concern of the business sector was to limit the size and scope of the local colonial administration. On the other hand, colonial officials argued that "of course" Hong Kong was a colony and as such it was required to make every possible effort to assume financial self-sufficiency.

The colonial government was not about to abandon opium as a potential source of revenue; taxes and regulations on opium might be revised and refined, but they would not be discarded. In an effort to improve revenues, the opium farm system was replaced in 1847 by opium licenses similar to those used for alcohol. The government's position was that by allowing opium to be sold by a number of licensed dealers, an element of competition would be introduced that would lower the price of opium in the marketplace. The result ought to have been more legal opium sales and a return of the Chinese junk traders to Hong Kong. Moreover, illicit sales of opium should also have decreased because many people would then be responsible for their discovery. In fact, however, the license system produced only 1867 British pounds in revenue in the first year of its operation and, despite optimistic forecasts to the contrary, continued to produce an average annual revenue of 1860 British pounds during the ten years it was in effect (Cheung, 1986:126). While competition may have served to lower the retail price, it was still higher than the price of illicit opium and under the license system no person or enforcement body was charged with the responsibility of discovery and confiscation of illicit drugs.

Legalization of the Opium Trade in Hong Kong

The Second Opium War (1856-58) and the signing of the Treaty of Tientsin (1858) legalized the opium trade in China and offered the British colonial government in Hong Kong the opportunity to make fundamental changes in its laws controlling the sale of opium locally. Now that opium no longer had to be smuggled into China, Hong Kong decided to remove all restraints on the sale of raw opium while retaining its right to tax imported prepared opium (known as *chandu*) consumed by Chinese residents in Hong Kong.

In order to effect these changes, the Opium Ordinance of 1844 was repealed and replaced by a new one (No. 2) in 1858. This ruling maintained the essential principle that the government could grant an opium monopoly to the highest bidder. All controls on the distribution of raw opium were removed, but sale and distribution of prepared opium, regardless of quantity or quality, now became a strict government monopoly. Deriving government revenue from prepared opium offered certain advantages. First, to prepare the drug clandestinely and remain undetected was difficult. This fact made the opium farmer's task of protecting his monopoly that much easier. Second, a strong demand for prepared opium existed within Hong Kong's Chinese community. Third, trade links with overseas Chinese communities in Australia and the U.S., where Hong Kong opium was highly regarded, made the monopoly even more attractive.

The new Opium Ordinance represented an attempt on the part of the colonial government to promote the wholesale trade in raw opium by doing away with all government interference. The government hoped that this move would stimulate Hong Kong's role as an important trading center. The ultimate effect, at least in relation to opium, was to consolidate Hong Kong's position as a major base for smuggling the drug into China. Unlike the Chinese ports and the "treaty ports" where opium was subject to a duty, Hong Kong's status as a British colony and free port meant that opium could enter Hong Kong free of import duties.[3] From Hong Kong it could then be shipped legally or, as was more likely the case, it could be smuggled into China. In either case, the Hong Kong government argued that it was not its responsibility to enforce Chinese laws regarding the importation of opium. As far as Hong Kong was concerned nothing illegal occurred as long as bills of purchase could be produced showing that raw opium had been legally purchased in Hong Kong. Eventually the situation became so serious that in 1868 the Chinese government set up a customs blockade of Hong Kong to stop the flow of illicit opium.

Despite the problems associated with the farming system, between 1858 and 1882 annual revenue increased from 4508 to 45 985 British pounds. In terms of total government revenue this represented a movement from 7% to 17%. Collusive bidding for the opium farm in 1883 resulted in a decline in government revenue and the decision to renew the licensing system. As before, this decision resulted in a huge decline in revenue. In 1886, a year after the government reinstated the monopoly system, revenues once again approached 40 000 British pounds. By 1887, Hong Kong derived 13% of its revenue from opium, and by 1889, this figure had increased to nearly 24%, or 94 257 British pounds. The Hong Kong government had finally begun to reap significant revenue from opium.

Increases in revenue in the late 1880s were not due to improvements in the administration of the farming system but rather to changes in Hong Kong's relations with China. During this period, for the first time, Hong Kong's colonial government co-operated with the Chinese government to control the trafficking in raw opium. With the implementation of provisions of the Chefoo Convention of July 1885, the colonial government agreed to keep accounts of the volume and value of the raw opium trade by establishing an Import and Export Office.[4] In return, China agreed to remove the customs blockade it had set up around Hong Kong in 1868.

Hong Kong drug legislation underwent dramatic reorganization in response to these changes. The Opium Ordinance of 1887 (No. 22) imposed restrictions on the possession and movement of raw and prepared opium. Movement of raw opium within the colony, except by those with a permit from the harbor master and signed by the opium farmer, was forbidden. From the standpoint of the opium farmer, the Opium Ordinance of 1887 had the added advantage that, if detected, all smuggled opium would be confiscated and returned to the opium farmer. The opium farmer was now in the enviable position of being able to smuggle opium without any fear of detection or loss of his opium. If his shipment was by some chance detected, the confiscated opium would, by law, be returned to him and he could try again or sell it through legitimate channels. Vast quantities of opium were smuggled into China from Hong Kong from 1888 onwards. This fact, plus the removal of the customs blockade, made the opium farm a truly attractive economic proposition. For the first time there was real competition for possession of the opium farm and the colonial government began to reap tremendous revenue from it. Opium was well on its way to becoming the most valuable source of revenue for the colonial government.[5]

The Rise of the Anti-Opium Movement

There are a number of possible explanations for the agitation against the opium trade in the nineteenth century. Anti-opium sentiment had been a feature of British political life since the 1840s, but to the extent that colonial rule in India was economically dependent on opium, Britain was inclined to go slow in reaction to China's demands that traffic in Indian opium be limited or eliminated.

In contrast, the United States, with a more limited involvement in the trade, used opium as a symbolic weapon against the better-established colonial powers in Asia in an attempt to expand American influence in the region. In 1908, ten years after the Philippines came under American rule, the U.S. placed a total ban on the importation, distribution, consumption, and smoking of opium. American initiative also lay behind the Shanghai Conference of 1909 which was designed to draw up recommendations to assist China in the anti-opium campaign it had launched in 1906.

At the conclusion of the Shanghai Conference, the U.S. issued invitations to yet another conference to draw up an international convention for regulation of opium and other dangerous drugs. This invitation resulted in Britain's signature to the Hague International Opium Convention of 1912, committing it to take measures for the "gradual and effective suppression of, the internal trade in, and use of, prepared opium" (cited in LaMotte, 1924:189). Provisions of the convention, promulgated after consultation with and agreement by the Hong Kong colonial government, restricted opium production and also extended to other drugs: morphine, cocaine, and heroin.

Hong Kong now was legally bound by treaty agreements to curtail the opium trade. The Opium Ordinance of 1887 had been in response to treaty requirements but its role had been entirely symbolic with its net effect an increase in the flow of opium to China and a rise in the value of the opium monopoly. The next major piece of Hong Kong drug legislation, the Opium Ordinance of 1909, banned the export of prepared opium from Hong Kong to China, prohibited its sale to women and to children under the age of 16, and closed Hong Kong's opium divans. The impetus for this ordinance derived from China's ongoing anti-opium campaign and the Shanghai Conference.

Following this piece of legislation, the Opium Ordinance of 1913 anticipated the provisions of the Hague Convention, placing further restrictions on the quantity of prepared opium that could be legally possessed by individuals. In 1914, partly in response to the Hague Convention and also for financial considerations, the Hong Kong government assumed control of the monopoly. Following the decision in 1909 to levy duties on alcohol, the Colonial Office agreed that Hong Kong should take over the opium monopoly. By 1915, Hong Kong derived 43% of its revenue from the sale of opium as compared to 34% in 1914 (Miners, 1983).

Under direct government control there was a steady rise in the value of opium to the Hong Kong government. Frequent advances in the retail price during the 1914-18 period were largely made feasible by the success of China's anti-opium campaign and the British cartel of opium merchants. This cartel had gained control of opium stocks that had accumulated in the "treaty ports" and Hong Kong after Indian auctions of opium to China had been suspended in 1913. Between 1914 and 1918, the retail price of one tael[6] of standard opium increased from HK$8.00 to $14.50, and by 1918 opium revenues were accounting for nearly 47% of the total revenue. The government justified these price increases on the grounds that high prices were necessary to restrict consumption (Miners, 1983:280).

The end of World War I brought renewed international efforts to control the distribution and use of opium and other addictive drugs. Again, the Americans took the lead and the newly-formed League of Nations assumed responsibility for enforcement of the provisions of the Hague Convention. In Hong Kong, however, these events were viewed with serious misgivings.

As Hong Kong entered the 1920s, new problems loomed on the horizon. China's anti-opium campaign began to break down under the pressure of ongoing civil disorder and a subsequent demand for increased government revenue. By 1920, China's growing supply of low-cost opium began to have an adverse impact on Hong Kong government opium sales; in the following year a vigorous campaign was launched in Hong Kong to halt the sale of illicit opium. The objective was not to suppress opium smoking, but to coerce addicts to purchase government opium. Between 1920 and 1921, the number of persons imprisoned for possession and use of illicit opium increased from 242 to 4036 (Miners, 1983:283).

By the early 1920s, the League of Nations had become the locus of pressure for an end to colonial opium monopolies. In 1923, one of the proposals for securing effective application of the Hague Convention was to limit the sale of opium to government shops, with smokers registered and issued ration cards. Governments in Europe's Far Eastern colonies were invited to establish local committees to consider these proposals and to make recommendations. The Hong Kong committee concluded that current measures would never lead to complete suppression and were effective only in holding opium usage at a reasonable level. In the committee's view, registration and rationing would lead to increased demand for smuggled opium and would merely encourage increased corruption in the police and customs departments. Hong Kong argued that the only real hope for complete suppression lay in decisions by China and other producing countries to cease the harvesting of opium poppies. Until this occurred, attempts to suppress would be "merely beating the air" (Sessional Papers 1924:60.)

In 1923, the first Dangerous Drugs Ordinance (No. 22) was passed in response to the requirements set in the 1912 International Opium Convention. The Dangerous Drugs Ordinance was directed at controlling the distribution and sale of morphine, heroin, cocaine, and medical opium. Noticeably absent from this list was prepared opium. However, given that prepared opium continued to be a source of considerable government revenue, this omission should come as no surprise. The Dangerous Drugs Ordinance was amended in 1928 to include "Indian hemp," and, in 1938, provisions against heroin were strengthened. Apart from these changes, however, the basic Dangerous Drugs Ordinance remained in effect until 1968, when it was repealed and replaced by a new ordinance (42 of 1968).[7]

The implementation of the Dangerous Drugs Ordinance in 1923 was entirely in line with the desire of the colonial government to continue to derive income from the sale of opium. It was also in line with previous legislation. In 1893, when morphine began to threaten government opium revenues, the response had been to quickly pass the Morphine Ordinance (No. 13) prohibiting the unauthorized sale and administration of morphine. The Dangerous Drugs Ordinance simply continued the principle of proscribing competing drugs on the grounds that they posed a danger to the community.

While events surrounding the control of opium in the 1920s and 1930s were complex, an overall pattern of government response by Hong Kong is discernible. There is no question that the colony was increasingly forced to respond to international demands for suppression of the opium trade. Hong Kong's position, supported even within the League of Nations, was that while it was willing to meet international demands to suppress opium use, any such policy was doomed to failure as long as China remained a source of cheap opium. It was a position the government continued to hold until the outset of World War II.

The decline in government revenue from opium in Hong Kong can be traced to two factors. First, there was the smuggling of illicit Chinese opium into the colony. The government periodically attempted to regain control of the local market by lowering the official price of opium. However, after an initial increase, sales inevitably declined in the face of even cheaper opium smuggled into the colony from China.[8]

A second factor affecting the decline of government revenue from opium was the spreading use of morphine and heroin. Considering opium's prominent role in providing revenue, the government was naturally concerned about the growing use of these other drugs. The Morphine Ordinance of 1893 had been passed to accomplish just such an end. Despite efforts at control, morphine and heroin use spread throughout China during the anti-opium movement and actively competed with opium in many parts of China. Government opium reports submitted to the League of Nations during the 1930s include repeated comments on the alarming spread of heroin (Reports on Opium and Dangerous Drugs 1932, 1936, 1938). Thus opium faced competition not just from cheap Chinese supplies but from morphine and heroin as well.

Conclusion

Opium's contribution to British rule in Hong Kong accounts for the colonial government's determination to resist international pressure supporting total abolition. More so than any other branch of the British government, the Colonial Office recognized the importance of the opium trade to the continuance of British rule; it was the one branch of government most responsive to the demands of the British colonial governors that the opium market be allowed to flourish. In the decades leading to World War II, the defense of the government's monopoly frequently included official lies. To this end, the colonial government produced two sets of opium accounts. One set, submitted to the League of Nations, showed that Hong Kong was experiencing heavy losses by maintaining the opium monopoly. This was accomplished by including the charges for police, hospitals, prisons, and the preventive service (forerunner of Hong Kong's

Customs and Excise Department) as part of the government's expenses. According to the government, the ultimate goal of the monopoly was total elimination of opium addiction at some unspecified date in the future. In a second set of accounts, submitted only to the British government, the costs included only the charges involved in processing and selling opium. This set of accounts more accurately reflected the true economic benefits of the monopoly to the colonial government.

Hong Kong's opium monopoly eventually came to an end in March 1943, when the U.S. government announced that it would ban all colonial opium monopolies in Japanese-occupied territories after re-occupation by American forces. The British government was in no position to object to America's demands. The fact that they were occupied by the Japanese pushed the financial considerations of maintaining colonies into the background and, in any case, there was no possibility of objections from British colonial governors. Consequently, the decision was made to prohibit totally the sale and distribution of opium on November 10, 1943, implemented by Proclamation 13 of the British Military Administration in September 1945. When British rule was re-established, the prohibition of opium and other drugs was implemented in Ordinances 5 and 20 of 1948. Opium was re-classified as a "dangerous drug" and put under the control of the Dangerous Drugs Ordinance. Since that date, Hong Kong has consistently followed a policy that totally restricts the sale and distribution of all drugs deemed dangerous to the public.

What lessons concerning the formation of law in European colonies can be drawn from the study of Hong Kong?

First, from Hong Kong's beginnings as a British colony, there was a pragmatic awareness that legal restrictions were an effective means to protect the opium monopoly from competing drugs. The government's primary interest was to find a way of making opium sales a reliable source of revenue.

Second, the aforementioned point helps to explain why Hong Kong adopted a punitive approach to the control of "dangerous drugs." Because the government's revenue base rested on opium, it was almost inevitable that Hong Kong would adopt a punitive approach to the control of "dangerous" (that is, competing) drugs. When the opium monopoly came to an end, opium was simply classified as another dangerous drug and consequently became subject to the provisions of the existing Dangerous Drugs Ordinance.

Third, it is clear that Hong Kong's colonial government was capable, when the occasion demanded, of pursuing policies in opposition to the interests of the business community and the wishes of the British government in London. There is considerable evidence that considerations of state survival and development have greatly influenced the fate of particular pieces of drug legislation in Hong Kong. Apparently, even in colonies, the state can and does act independently if its direct interests are at stake.

Fourth, colonies are especially sensitive to outside pressures due to their economic and political dependence. The formation of law in colonies tend to be more reactive or defensive than in Western societies. In the case of opium laws in Hong Kong, we have seen a long history of the colonial government adapting to shifting relations between China, Britain, and the U.S. Opium policy in Hong Kong was shaped first by the British government's desire to establish effective colonial rule in Hong Kong and European hegemony in China, and later by the efforts of the U.S. to counteract European influence in East Asia in order to establish itself as a leading power in the region. Opium legislation in Hong Kong ultimately reflects these external realities.

Notes

1. Hong Kong is organized politically along lines traditionally associated with British colonies. The colonial government, with a governor as its titular head, is served by an Executive Council, which advises him on important policy matters, and a Legislative Council, which enacts legislation and controls public expenditures. Until recently, all members of both bodies were appointed.

2. The retail sale of opium had indirectly been taxed since the establishment of Hong Kong. A public market was let out at a fixed rate, and retail transactions in opium and other types of commodities were confined to this mart. The government derived revenue from the trade by renting stalls, but the resulting income was so small as to be considered insignificant. With this exception, during the 1841-44 period, the Hong Kong government derived revenue directly from the sale of land leases and licenses to public houses.

3. In addition to establishing Hong Kong as a British colony, the Treaty of Nanking (1842) set up five "treaty ports" in China: Canton, Amoy, Foochow, Ningpo, and Shanghai. These ports were specifically established to encourage foreign commerce and residence in China, as well as to assure that a fair and regular tariff was levied on trade.

4. In 1875, Britain seized the opportunity provided by an attack on a British delegation and the murder of a British officer in China to press the Chinese authorities for improved foreign relations and additional protection of trade. Essentially this involved revising the Treaty of Tientsin. The result was the Chefoo Convention which was ratified in 1885. An article of the Convention directed the appointment of a commission in 1886 to examine opium smuggling from Hong Kong to China. One of the outcomes of this commission was the recommendation that Hong Kong should co-operate with China in the control of smuggling.

5. The dramatic rise in the farm's value can be seen by the fact that the average income per year increased from 38 000 British pounds in 1876-86 to over 80 000 in 1887-97.

6. A tael is a measure of weight, which in China is equal to 1/16 catty or 1.33 ounce (37.8 g). It was also used as a unit of money in China, being equal in value to one tael of silver.

7. Opium was not included in the first Dangerous Drugs Ordinance. However, opium was still controlled by the Opium Ordinance, and this Ordinance operated in tandem with the Dangerous Drugs Ordinance until it was repealed by British Military Administration Proclamation No. 13 of 1945.

8. The Hong Kong government decided, in 1927, to compete head-to-head with smugglers by reducing the price of government opium and by selling even cheaper blends of confiscated Persian and Chinese opium. Sales of government opium immediately tripled, and demand quickly outstripped supply. The government's attempts to procure additional stocks from Persia were disallowed by the British government.

References

Becker, Howard S. 1963. *Outsiders: Studies in the Sociology of Deviance*. New York: Free Press.

Bonnie, Richard J. and Charles H. Whitebread. 1974. *The Marijuana Conviction*. Charlottesville: University of Virginia Press.

Cheung, Lucy Tsiu-ping. 1986. The Opium Monopoly in Hong Kong, 1844-1887. Hong Kong: University of Hong Kong, M.Phil. Dissertation.

Colonial Records Office. 1843. "Further Instructions to Sir H. Pottinger on Affairs in Hong Kong." In *Government Dispatches and Replies from Secretaries of State for the Colonies*. Series 129, 3:67-77.

Dickson, Donald T. 1968. "Bureaucracy and Morality: An Organizational Perspective on a Moral Crusade." *Social Problems* 16:143-156.

Fields, Albert and Peter Tararin. 1970. "Opium in China." *British Journal of Addiction* 64:371-382.

Fitzpatrick, Peter. 1980. *Law and the State in Papua New Guinea*. London: Academic Press.

Galliher, John F. and Allyn Walker. 1977. "The Puzzle of the Marijuana Tax Act of 1937." *Social Problems* 24:367-376.

Huggins, Martha. 1985. *From Slavery to Vagrancy in Brazil: Crime and Social Control in the Third World*. New Brunswick, NJ: Rutgers University Press.

LaMotte, Ellen N. 1924. *The Ethics of Opium*. New York: Century Company.

Lindesmith, Alfred R. 1959. "Federal Law and Drug Addiction." *Social Problems* 7:48-57.

———. 1965. *The Addict and the Law*. Bloomington: Indiana University Press.

Miners, Norman. 1983. "The Hong Kong Government Opium Monopoly, 1914-1941." *Journal of Imperial and Commonwealth History* 11:275-299.

Musto, David F. 1973. *The American Disease: Origins of Narcotic Control*. New Haven: Yale University Press.

Parliamentary Papers. 1971. *British Parliamentary Papers: Opium War and Opium Trade*, Vol. 31. Shannon: Irish University Press.

Reasons, Charles. 1974. *The Criminologist: Crime and the Criminal*. Pacific Palisades, CA: Goodyear.

Reports on Opium and Dangerous Drugs. 1932. *Report of the Government of Hong Kong on the Traffic in Opium and Dangerous Drugs*. Hong Kong: Government Printer and Publishers.

Select Committee. 1847. *Report from the Select Committee on Commercial Relations with China*. London: House of Commons. Reprinted in *British Parliamentary Papers: Commercial Relations*, Vol. 38. Shannon: Irish University Press, 1971.

Sessional Papers. 1924. "Report of the Committee Appointed by H.E. The Governor to Consider the Colony's Position with Regard to the Obligations Incurred Under the International Opium Convention, 1912." *Hong Kong Legislative Council* 7:59-64.

Sumner, Colin. 1982. *Crime, Justice and Underdevelopment*. London: Heinemann.

Part III

Future Directions

9

Illegal Drugs: Where We Stand and What We Can Do

John F. Galliher

The United States is the most forceful magnet for illegal drugs in the world. And it must from the outset be recognized that it is largely beyond the scope of the law to explain why this is true. We assume that historical, cultural, and economic factors are more important than the law in creating this problem. Moreover, there is no reason to give any legitimacy to our existing legal controls since they have never been based on scientific demonstrations of a drug's dangers but rather on racism. Musto (1973), for example, demonstrates that the strongest support for the legal prohibition of drugs is when the substance in question has been associated with some threatening minority group. Certain drugs have been feared because of their alleged effects on specific minorities, purportedly making these groups more difficult to control. Cocaine was associated in the public mind with lawless blacks, opium with sexually aggressive Chinese, and marijuana with violent Mexicans.

Since the law can be demonstrated to be both ineffective in controlling use and based on racism, in an earlier paper total legalization of all drugs was recommended (Galliher, 1988). A growing number of American public officials agree (*New York Times*, 1988a). Sentiment along these lines is apparently developing in the United Kingdom (*The Economist*, 1988). To continue without major adjustments to our nation's narcotics control policies is unthinkable. Indeed, the magnitude of the problem is so great as to affect even foreign policy decisions, as exemplified by U.S. government dealings with drug pushers among the Nicaraguan Contras and General Noriega of Panama.

Earlier, Chambliss (1977:60) found that to encourage anti-communism in Southeast Asia the U.S. Central Intelligence Agency (CIA) had allowed friendly tribesmen to grow and traffic in opium and even itself became "a major trafficker in the international narcotics industry." On the home front the American Bar Association has recently noted that drug cases are overwhelming the U.S. court system (*Columbia Daily Tribune*, 1988c). American prisons also are awash with such offenders. Currently, 30% of all state prisoners enter institutions on drug charges (*Christian Science Monitor*, 1988b). All of these rationales notwithstanding, when I made proposals for drug legalization I provided no recommendations about how this might be politically feasible (Galliher, 1988).

To begin any discussion of drug controls, the first question involves the issue of delineating the specific problem drugs in the U.S. today, since the types of legal solutions that have been advanced pertaining to drug abuse have depended to a great extent on the specific substances being considered. A distinction has been made (National Research Council, 1982) between total prohibition of supply and use, and partial prohibition of supply only. This distinction provides a starting point for assessing the possible legal approaches that have been made with respect to drugs. Here I will propose some practical, reasoned, and gradual steps which the U.S. government could take to deal with the problem, keeping in mind relevant political and cultural factors.

Alcohol

The alcohol industry is an important part of the U.S. economy and it is widely agreed by Americans of almost all political stripes that the American experiment with criminal prohibition of alcohol was a failure. There are currently no signs of a decline in America's prodigious appetite for alcohol. While it is widely recognized that alcohol claims millions of lives each year, it is also recognized that this is above the law and can only be controlled, if at all, through education. This drug is associated with a considerable amount of the violence in the U.S., being present in a high percentage of those who commit murder, as well as massively involved in much of the tragic loss of life through auto accidents. The only controls here are that in most American states the purchaser must be over 21 years old, and that widely increasing attempts to prevent and punish driving "under the influence" are being made. Yet even these reasonable and modest law enforcement regulations have been less than a success due to slack enforcement of age restrictions and because drinking-and-driving is so closely associated in American culture. Most Americans drive to taverns or drive to cocktail parties and think nothing about driving home after a long evening of drinking. It is especially interesting to note, as we will below, the types of drugs and drug controls being considered where political officials remind us of the historical failure to control alcohol use.

Tobacco

Another drug problem of massive proportions is revealed by the U.S. Surgeon General's recent announcement that cigarettes are addictive (*New York Times*, 1988b). This drug is known to be responsible for the illness and death of millions of Americans every year, victims of lung cancer, emphysema, and cardio-vascular disease. Thus tobacco commercials have been banned from television and health warnings must appear in all printed advertising and on tobacco packages.

Even in the face of this apparent danger, the U.S. Congress pumps massive amounts of tax dollars into tobacco farming every year to insure that tobacco farmers will make a suitable profit from their labors. The Agricultural Adjustment Act of 1938 is one of several federal tobacco support programs. Under this act, low-interest loans are made to tobacco growers on the condition that production be limited, thus providing price support at specific levels. The program has grown and in 1986 (*ASCS Commodity Fact Sheet*, 1986a:2), for example, the Department of Agriculture reported that with flue-cured tobacco "On July 1, 1986, 790 million pounds of flue-cured tobacco valued at $2031 million were held under government loan." And for burley tobacco (*ASCS Commodity Fact Sheet*, 1986b:1) "As of July 1, 1986, 354 million pounds of burley tobacco valued at $915 million were held under government loan." Thus, for just these two types of tobacco alone, approximately 3 billion U.S. dollars in federal funds were committed in this one year. Only in the last several months have the American courts begun to hold cigarette manufacturers financially responsible for the death and disease they cause (*New York Times*, 1988c). Yet children of any age can purchase cigarettes from millions of public machines. No law enforcement is used in controlling this particularly dangerous drug. And if anyone suggests the prohibition of cigarette sales, the failure of alcohol prohibition is always mentioned.

Amphetamines and Barbiturates

Here we have addictive, mind-altering and life-threatening drugs that are legal and can be prescribed by physicians (Graham, 1972). These drugs are legal because they are thought to be used by good people for good purposes, to help them work or sleep better. As with tobacco, law enforcement is seldom used to control these dangerous drugs even though it was reported that more than 1300 persons died in 1977 from overdoses of barbiturates (U.S. Department of Justice, 1977). Any attempt to legally control the use of these substances is doomed to failure because it conflicts with huge corporate drug profits. In the case of amphetamines, eight to ten billion of these pills are sold legally each year even though there are few known medical uses for them. Moreover, massive amounts of legally manufactured amphetamines are illegally diverted to the black market. The failure to control this drug is due to the powerful lobby of the drug manufacturers who have been demonstrated to control all legislative efforts (Graham, 1972).

Marijuana

Among the illegal drugs, marijuana is by far the most widely used. As recently as 1977, a clear majority of teenagers admitted to having at least tried it once (Abelson and Fishburne, 1977). In spite of this widespread use, in 1977 there were reports of only one marijuana overdose death (U.S. Department of Justice, 1977). By 1984 there were reports of 18 marijuana overdose deaths, three by suicide — all a medical impossibility (National Institute on Drug Abuse, 1984). In any case, because of marijuana's bulkiness compared to many other illegal drugs, its control represents the easiest for law enforcement. The plants are often very large and when growing in open fields can often be spotted easily from the air. When being smuggled, the packages are generally much bulkier than in the cases of cocaine and heroin. This produces news reports that seem very dramatic, such as "11 Tons of Pot Seized in Giant Coast 'Bust'," (*Jackson Daily News*, 1976), and "20 Tons of Pot Seized off N.C. River," (*News and Observer*, 1978).

But it is widely recognized that, even with all our attempts at legal suppression, marijuana remains one of our nation's most lucrative cash crops. Just prior to decriminalization of marijuana in California, it was estimated that enforcement costs were U.S. $100 million annually (California Senate Committee, 1974). Nationwide, over 400 000 Americans are arrested each year for marijuana offenses (U.S. Department of Justice, 1985) at an estimated cost of U.S.$5 billion (NORML, 1986). Even with all of these expenditures, there are very few convictions handed down for marijuana offenders. Most American states which have not formally decriminalized possession of marijuana have only a handful of inmates in their prisons for this offense, making the conviction of the few who are imprisoned seem even more discriminatory (Galliher et al., 1988). Continued prohibition thus leads to revenue lost to corporations that could otherwise profit from marijuana's legal production and sale, and tax revenues lost to government, as well as diversion of law enforcement that could be used to fight life-threatening drugs. And because marijuana is illegal it cannot be used for the treatment of the effects of glaucoma and multiple sclerosis, as well as nausea from chemotherapy in cancer patients. This leads to the truly ridiculous case of a cancer patient in Kentucky recently convicted of possession of seven and a half ounces of marijuana which, according to the testimony of physicians, he needed to prevent starvation caused by the nausea and vomiting typically associated with cancer treatment. As a conciliatory move he was fined only $1 and not jailed on the condition that he complete a drug teatment program. The judge ultimately suspended even the fine but not the mandatory drug abuse rehabilitation program (*Columbia Daily Tribune*, 1988a; 1988b).

Former U.S. Presidents Ford (*Columbus Evening Dispatch*, 1974) and Carter (*New York Times*, 1977), together with a number of American state legislators, have recognized that marijuana is like alcohol in the sense that when a majority of affluent Americans desire to use a given drug it becomes a candidate for decriminalization.

There is widespread evidence of a law enforcement failure here, so much so that 11 states decriminalized marijuana possession during the 1970s and retain only nominal civil fines. In many states there is *de facto* decriminalization with virtually a total abeyance of arrest and prosecution for marijuana possession (Galliher et al., 1988).

Heroin

While heroin use may be decreasing, there is no evidence this is a consequence of law enforcement efforts. In the early 1970s, New York State attempted to reduce the use of heroin by (1) reducing prosecutors' discretion to bargain with defendants for guilty pleas in exchange for reduced legal liability, (2) drastically increasing mandatory minimum penalties in such cases, and (3) hiring many new judges — all without evidence of success (New York Joint Committee, 1978). Experience strongly suggests that the heroin supply in the streets failed to diminish. Street prices for heroin did not go up, overdose deaths from the drug did not go down, but convictions for heroin sales declined. Police, judges, prosecutors, and juries were simply unwilling to impose tough penalties. So dramatic was the failure that after only three years the law was significantly amended.

In the late 1980s, the drug of choice on the streets increasingly became cocaine and "crack," replacing heroin. In 1977, it was reported that there were 1262 deaths from heroin overdose (U.S. Department of Justice, 1977), but more recently there has been some evidence of a declining law enforcement need. In 1979, only 619 were reported to have died from heroin overdoses and in 1984 this figure had risen slightly to 1072 (U.S. Department of Justice, 1979; National Institute on Drug Abuse, 1984). In short, there is no evidence of sizeable increases in the use of heroin. As with marijuana, heroin cannot be used legally in the U.S. to kill the horrific pain of terminal cancer patients even though it is well known to be more effective than other drugs, and in fact is used for this purpose in the United Kingdom (CBS News, 1984).

Cocaine and "Crack"

Today cocaine and "crack" are seen as the biggest health and law enforcement problem in the U.S. In 1977 it was reported that only

54 Americans had died from cocaine overdose. However, this figure had risen to 141 in 1979 (U.S. Department of Justice, 1979) and 604 in 1984 (National Institute on Drug Abuse, 1984). In the face of this problem the Reagan Administration has suggested urine testing for all federal employees. It is mainly due to the threat of cocaine that today we find the routine urine testing of university athletes. The fact that university athletes are tested and not university medical school surgeons is not based on demonstrated need but apparently on racism. One might ask what the consequences are if an athlete enters a game under the influence of illegal drugs. The worst that can happen is that the school will lose a game. If a surgeon enters an operating room in a similar condition the worst that can happen is that the patient will lose his or her life.

It was the increasing threat of crack that prompted the Reagan Administration to begin the much-maligned and short-lived "zero tolerance" program, which included the seizure of vessels at sea when even a seed of marijuana was found. This particular law enforcement program was quickly modified after several multi-million dollar yachts were seized on such grounds. The use of the American military was also planned in the "war" against drugs. War analogies aside, the argument is that since drug use affects our national security it is appropriate to use the military in fighting the traffic of illegal drugs. The problem is that the military has neither the equipment nor the proper training for such law enforcement and will surely be diverted from tasks it is trained to perform. Other highly questionable recommendations found in proposed federal legislation include the death penalty for drug pushers and relaxation of the rules of evidence in order to secure more convictions in drug cases. Before supporting calls for draconian penalty increases we should remember the debacle in the state of New York.

Summary: Available Law Enforcement Alternatives

In the case of tobacco, the most positive environmental support is found in government subsidies for producers combined with a total absence of legal controls on possession and use (Table 1). Next most positive is the current program for the control of alcohol. Here we find an absence of criminal penalties for production and sale as well as for possession and use. The only controls are poorly enforced drunk-driving laws and legal age restrictions for purchase.

Barbiturates and amphetamines also are produced without criminal controls and are widely available through physicians' prescriptions. Prohibition of alcohol was an historical experiment with the prohibition of production and sale but provided no penalties for possession and use. More extreme than the experiment with alcohol prohibition is the control of marijuana which provides criminal penalties for production and sale and usually either civil penalties (small fines) or no enforcement of any kind (de facto decriminalization) for use and possession. The extreme in prohibition is reached in the case of heroin and cocaine where both sale and possession are controlled by criminal penalties. Since the U.S. government is obviously grasping at straws, perhaps in this environment ideas that were heretofore considered wildly radical and irresponsible, can, for the first time, be seriously considered.

Table 1   Methods of Controlling Supply and Use of Drugs

Drug	Response to supplying	Legal control of use and possession
Tobacco	Stimulated and taxed	Public machines
Alcohol	Regulated and taxed	Available to adults
Barbiturates & Amphetamines	Regulated and taxed	By prescription
Marijuana	Criminal penalties	Decriminalization or criminal penalties
Cocaine & Heroin	Criminal penalties	Criminal penalties

A Proposal for Gradual Reduction of Penalties and Research Assessment

It is easy to see that many drug control policies have been irrational and counterproductive. We can only hope that it will be possible in the future to develop more effective solutions by treating drugs appropriately on the basis of their actual danger and risk to society. Seemingly punitive laws have created a massive untaxed financial empire which has demonstrated the capacity to corrupt police, customs agents, judges, and other officials. Given the high cost of these drugs, whose value is a product of the risk involved, they are estimated by police officials to be responsible for a high percentage of armed robbery and burglary. Addicts commit such offenses to purchase their drugs. And these laws breed disrespect for the law in general, specifying as they do harsh penalties for relatively mild substances such as marijuana and legal access to addictive, mind-altering drugs such as amphetamines. Although there is some debate about its effectiveness, over the years the British government, by allowing addicts to secure drugs legally at government clinics (Lindesmith, 1965), has avoided at least some of the problems of drug abuse.

Perhaps there could be gradual decriminalization, using only civil fines for controls, followed by legalization. Usage levels could be monitored after each change were implemented. As a part of a federal program attempts may be made to involve specific states by altering state laws on a trial basis in return for special federal funds to be used for medical treatment and education. The federal government might attempt decriminalization of cocaine and crack under federal law in selected state laws, combined with a massive education and medical treatment program in targeted states. Then the state and federal governments could monitor the number of overdose deaths and use patterns for one year in these experimental states, through use of anonymous survey data and comparison to existing baseline data available from annual surveys of drug use conducted by Rand (see, for example, Abelson and Fishburne, 1977; Fishburne, 1979). Comparisons can also be made to similar information in those states not experimenting with their laws. Assuming no massive increases in cocaine and crack use patterns after one year, total legalization could then be tried, followed again by a year of research evaluation of use patterns.

If there are massive increases in overdose deaths or in the use of cocaine or crack during either the trial period of decriminalization or legalization, the research design should allow identification of the precise type of users involved. Presumably this will allow the generation of intelligent social policy and legislative reactions. If increases occur mainly among the very young, this may call for a different legislative reaction than if older citizens are involved. And if the increases are isolated to one state, or one type of state, or to one type of neighborhood across all states, then again, presumably, social policy can take this into account.

After cocaine and crack, the next drug to challenge might be marijuana or perhaps even heroin. Again, first decriminalization could be tried, followed by a year of research and then, assuming no large increases, the next step could be legalization. Evidence suggests, however, that such experimentation may be unnecessary with regard to marijuana. In the 1970s, 11 states decriminalized the possession of this drug with no evidence of consequent increases in use (Johnston et al., 1981). By this gradual process the use of heroin, LSD, cocaine, and marijuana can be potentially removed from the law enforcement arena and treated as medical problems to the degree that they do represent medical problems threatening the lives of users. The final solution then involves the legalization of both possession and sale of all the drugs discussed here. It is increasingly recognized that there can be no sensible legal distinctions between possession and sale. As with alcohol and barbiturates, the government could control the purity and strength of drugs sold legally, and could also determine the prices of these drugs as well as age limits for purchase, although this last problem will always be difficult to enforce. Such efforts would free law enforcement authorities to focus on crimes of violence such as rape, murder, and armed robbery where there is overwhelming consensus that the laws should be enforced. Finally, the advantage of such a program is that all the answers need not be known before alternatives are tried including, as this recommendation does, an ongoing research component.

In a recent editorial, the *Christian Science Monitor* (1988a) disagreed with proposals for the decriminalization even of marijuana because this would send a "mixed message to youth" and make access "freer." However, stiff penalties not imposed also send a "mixed message." Perhaps even prior to the research proposed above, analysis of the experience of the 11 states that decriminalized marijuana during the 1970s could be instructive to determine whether access is indeed freer than in culturally similar neighboring states where decriminalization has not been enacted. Recently, during a televised debate on the legalization of drugs, the American Broadcasting Corporation's medical consultant, Dr. Tim Johnson, summarized the comments of those who had spoken on both sides of the issue (ABC News, 1988):

> I think the word legalization implies too much moral abdication
> to the drug problem to ever become politically acceptable in this

country. But I do feel that we're going to have to find some of the middle ground . . . in between a pure criminal approach on the one hand and a legalization approach on the other. That involves more emphasis on the medical-therapeutic model and less emphasis on the criminal-punishment model. That will have to be done carefully and very selectively. But obviously the extremes in most instances don't work . . . We do have to try to find the middle ground.

Presumably how far we can go with such changes will become clear from the ongoing research suggested here. This is a plea to involve researchers in gathering the facts of the situation, rather than to continue to allow politicians to make these decisions on the basis of their personal or political prejudices, independent of empirical reality.

References

Abelson, Herbert I. and Patricia M. Fishburne. 1977. *National Survey on Drug Abuse*. Rockville, MD: National Institute on Drug Abuse.

ASCS Commodity Fact Sheet (Agriculture Stabilization and Conservation Service). 1986a. "Flue-Cured Tobacco, Summary of 1986 Support Program," U.S. Department of Agriculture, August.

———. 1986b. "Burley Tobacco, Summary of 1986 Support Program," U.S. Department of Agriculture, December.

American Broadcasting Corporation (ABC) News. 1988. "The Legalization of Drugs," National Town Meeting, September 13.

California Senate Committee of Control of Marihuana. 1974. *Understanding the Social Costs of Marihuana*. Sacramento: February 14.

Chambliss, William J. 1977. "Markets, Profits, Labor and Smack," *Contemporary Crises* 1 January: 53-75.

Columbia Broadcasting System (CBS) News. 1984. 60 Minutes. "Just What the Doctor Ordered," December 2.

Columbia Daily Tribune (Missouri). 1988a. "Cancer Patient Fined $1 on Pot Charge," June 30: 10.

———. 1988b. "$1 Pot Fine Suspended for Cancer Patient," August 4: 2.

———. 1988c. "Drug War Overloads Entire Justice System, December 3: 8.

Columbus Evening Dispatch (Ohio). 1974. "Pot Statement Expected," November 15: B9.

Christian Science Monitor. 1988a. "Don't Decriminalize Drugs," December 8: 15.

———. 1988b. "Rise in Drug Offenses Crams Prisons," December 13: 3-4.

Fishburne, Patricia M., Herbert I. Abelson, and Ira Cisin. 1979. *National Survey on Drug Abuse: Main Findings*. Rockville, MD: National Institute on Drug Abuse.

Galliher, John F. 1988. "Legal Control of Drug Abuse: Past Prejudices, Present Problems and Future Prospects," pp. 25-33 in *Perspectives in Drug Abuse, Vol. 1*. J.M. Scher and M. Segal (eds.), London: Freund Publishing House, Ltd.

Galliher, John F., Albert Dichiara and Steven E. Murphy. 1988. "The Origins of Marihuana Decriminalization: An Unfinished Reform," paper read at the Annual Meetings of the American Sociological Association, Atlanta.

Graham, James M. 1972. "Amphetamine Politics on Capitol Hill," *Transaction* 9 (January): 14-22, 53.

Jackson Daily News (Mississippi). 1976. "11 Tons of Pot Seized in Giant Coast 'Bust,'" October 4.

Johnston, Lloyd D., Patrick M. O'Malley and Jerald G. Bachman. 1981. Marihuana Decriminalization: The Impact on Youth, 1975-1980. Monitoring the Future, Occasional Paper, No. 13.

Lindesmith, Alfred R. 1965. *The Addict and the Law*. Bloomington: Indiana University Press.

Musto, David F. 1973. *The American Disease: Origins of Narcotic Control*. New Haven: Yale University Press.

National Institute on Drug Abuse. 1984. *Annual Data Statistical Series*. Washington, D.C.: U.S. Government Printing Office.

National Research Council. 1982. *An Analysis of Marihuana Policy*. Washington, D.C.: National Academy Press.

New York Joint Committee on Drug Law Evaluation. 1978. *Executive Summary*. Washington, D.C.: National Institute of Law Enforcement and Criminal Justice.

New York Times. 1977. "Carter Asks Congress to Decriminalize Marihuana Possession; Cocaine Law is Studied," March 15: 15 (Section 1).

———. 1988a. "Growing Number of Public Officials and Scholars Call for Debate on Question of Making Drugs Legal," May 15: 1 (Section 1).

———. 1988b. "Surgeon General C. Everette Koop in Annual Report on Smoking and Health, Warns that Nicotine is as Addictive as Heroin and Cocaine," May 17: 1 (Section 1).

———. 1988c. "Federal Jury in Newark Finds Liggett Group at Least Partially Liable in Lung-Cancer Death of Rose Cippollone, Smoker for 40 Years," June 14: 1 (Section 1).

News and Observer (Raleigh, North Carolina). 1978. "20 Tons of Pot Seized off N.C. River," February 6.

NORML. 1986. "Marihuana and Justice," pp. 6-7 in *Common Sense for America*. Washington, D.C.: National Organization for the Reform of Marihuana Laws.

The Economist. 1988. "Getting Gangsters Out of Drugs," pp. 9-10, April 2.

U. S. Department of Justice. 1977. *Project DAWN.* Washington, D.C.: Drug Enforcement Administration.

————. 1979. *Project DAWN.* Washington, D.C.: Drug Enforcement Administration.

————. 1985. *FBI Uniform Crime Reports.* Washington, D.C.: U.S. Government Printing Office.

Index